Celebrated quilt artist Sandra Meech's last book, *Connecting Art to Stitch*, explored the ways in which fine-art concepts can be taken into stitch to make outstanding pieces of quilt art. In this exciting new title, the author turns her attention to the rules of design, and how they can be harnessed to inform exciting new stitched textiles and art quilts. You will learn how to recognize good composition, and the essential principles and elements of design that all textile artists need to know. The author's signature practical exercises help you translate these rules into your own textile work, stimulating your creativity and encouraging you to explore new textures, materials and techniques. Detailed analyses of textile artists' work provide an invaluable breakdown of how design rules can be applied.

Packed with a huge range of images from the finest quilt and textile artists working today, this beautiful book is a must-have for anyone who wants to create better textile art.

Connecting
Design to Stitch

Connecting
Design to Stitch

Sandra Meech

BATSFORD

Acknowledgements

I would like to thank the many textile friends and students everywhere who have offered continued support and inspiration over the years. Thank you too to my colleagues in Quilt Art, Studio 21 and Connections who have generously allowed me to share their excellent work, and to Michael Wicks for great photography. My biggest appreciation goes to my family, especially Darryl for his help and encouragement in all aspects of my textile career.

First published in the United Kingdom in 2012 by
Batsford
10 Southcombe Street
London
W14 0RA

An imprint of Anova Books Company Ltd

ISBN 978 1 84994 024 5

A CIP catalogue for this book is available from the British Library.

21 20 19 18 17 16 15 14 13 12
10 9 8 7 6 5 4 3 2 1

Reproduction by Rival Colour Ltd, UK
Printed and bound by 1010 Printing International Ltd, China

This book can be ordered direct from the publisher at www.anovabooks.com, or try your local bookshop.

Page 1: **West Bay 1** (Sandra Meech, UK). Collage with stitch. Page 2: **Icebreak (detail)** (Sandra Meech UK). Page 3: **Meltdown 2** (Sandra Meech, UK). Left: **Boats at West Bay** (Sandra Meech, UK). Digital photo image with acrylic. Opposite: **Beach on the Cape** (Sandra Meech, UK). Stitched mixed-media collage with photo inspiration.

CONTENTS

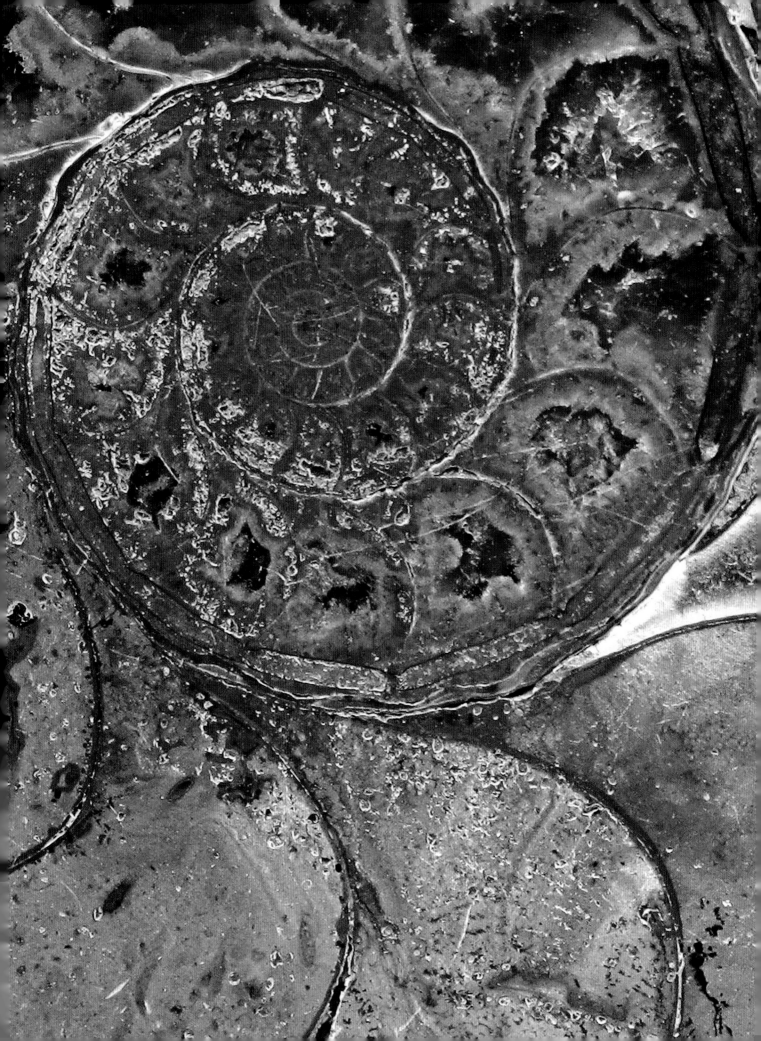

HOW TO USE THIS BOOK

Connecting Design to Stitch is an essential guide to design and composition for the contemporary stitched-textile artist. Exploring your own personal themes and styles through composition exercises and design classes can enable you to discover a new direction or create a fresh series of work. Inspiration from realism – landscape, still life, architecture, travels, city life, people and cultures, or details and textures in nature – could become a source of research, and working expressively in abstract might become a new way forward. If you come from traditional patchwork and quilting or embroidery, approaching textiles as an artist can encourage you to move out of your comfort zone and explore new ways in which to express yourself.

Within this book we will consider the importance of photography for observing and recording information and practising composition through the lens. Taking pictures can help you to identify centres of interest and find details you hadn't noticed before in the world around you, while the use of basic photo-editing methods on your computer can impact your design decisions. Working with collage can also be a rich source of inspiration for textile artists. Using painted paper, black-and-white and colour photocopies and cloth as surfaces for collage can help you consolidate your ideas. I have tried to keep surface methods simple – there is so much attention given to new materials, products and stitch embellishment it is easy to become overwhelmed. And while new products and techniques can help you to create interesting effects, they do not necessarily make the final work a considered textile piece. Too much attention to elaborate surfaces should not compromise the good use of colour and design. *Less is more.*

There are different ways in which to use this reference book. As a self-study guide, it allows you to work on your ideas alone, at your own pace. Alternatively, you can work through the exercises contained in this book with a group of friends – it is amazing how we each can enjoy the same challenge in dramatically different ways. Each design class provides an endless number of possibilities for future work. As a course of study, your progress through this book can become a map of your journey through the principles and elements – the building blocks – of design and composition, and you will gain confidence along the way.

By breaking down design into different styles (for example, painting, sculpture or graphic design), we can look at the impact each has had on stitched textiles, both historically and in contemporary practice. In each case, direct links to fabric and stitch are made and illustrated by the work of contemporary artists. The more you analyse composition, the more design becomes second nature and, as your skills and understanding of composition develop, you will be able to tell instantly and instinctively when and why a textile piece works.

There is something for everyone in these pages, whatever level of art or stitch discipline you come from. Containing composition and design suggestions, and examples that explore various themes, this book can become a valuable reference, guide and workbook for future projects. While there is no quick fix for achieving great compositions, with practice and a sound understanding of the principles and elements of design, everyone can create well composed, consolidated and dynamic textile art.

Left: Ammonite showing one of nature's design sequences (photo: Sandra Meech, UK).

Top right: Detail of image shown on page 49. Bottom right: Spiral marks on cloth (both Sandra Meech, UK).

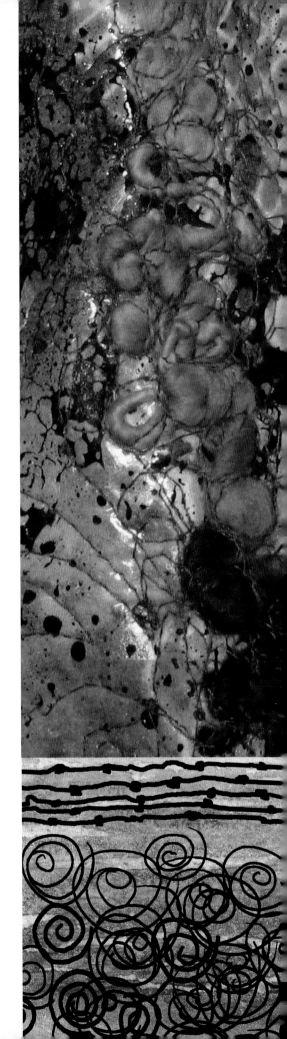

DESIGN

A few years ago the word 'design' might have inspired fear and trepidation among many quilters and embroiderers, but times are changing. Contemporary textiles are now seen in galleries, community spaces, open competitions and exhibitions and, of course, on the Internet. It is exciting to see that more textile artists and students are applying art and design practice and stretching the boundaries in fibre art and stitched textiles. When stitched textiles are taken into the realm of art, it is essential that they also include good composition and design.

Left: **Northwest Passage** (Sandra Meech, UK).
This painting, based on a high-horizon
composition, includes image transfer and
directional stitch marks worked in wool.
Right: **Polar Meltdown** (Sandra Meech, UK).
A dimensional mixed-media fabric collage
with added copper.

Natural creativity or sense of design is something that I believe is in all of us. Evident in children, it becomes submerged by other influences as we grow up. There are many people who can automatically place shapes on a surface in interesting and dynamic ways, while others struggle with the challenge. However, we can all find the confidence to explore new ways of expression in fabric and stitch – styles that move beyond the 30cm (12in) block for a bed quilt or the traditional embroidered motif and into the realms of expressive art textiles.

The word 'design' is used liberally in the disciplines of fine art, advertising, architecture, textiles, interior design and graphic design. We all know the visual differences between these disciplines but, essentially, they have a great deal in common when it comes to design. (How different design styles in the world around us can greatly influence our personal approach to design is discussed in full in chapter 2.) Good design, composition and colour choices in any discipline have the power to captivate the viewer immediately. When it comes to textile art, the composition should work at a distance of 3m (10ft) to pique the viewer's interest, encouraging them to move closer to the piece to enjoy the details (piecing, stitching, textures or embellishment across the surface) in a more complete way. If the work does not engage the viewer from that distance, no amount of time spent on surface techniques or precise stitching matters – they will simply move on.

Top left: **Polar Meltdown 1, 2, 3**; left: **Polar Meltdown 1**; above: **Polar Meltdown 2 (detail)** (all Sandra Meech, UK). These are all high-horizon landscape compositions in relief, with fabric collage stitched through Wireform with copper shim.

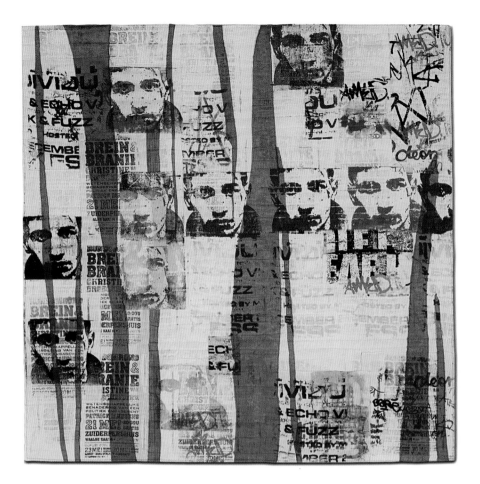

Left: **White Wall 9** (Jette Clover, Belgium). The linear marks contrast with the horizontal repeat of the face images, and the red accent creates movement. Detail shown above. Below: **Thameside** (Sandra Meech, UK). The inspiration for this piece came from blocks of pavement and the horizontal and vertical shapes seen from Tate Modern, London.

Through practice and understanding of the elements and principles of design, stronger compositions will be made. Recognizing ways in which to engage the viewer in our work with the placement of shape, colour and line are invaluable. It takes practice for good design to become intuitive but, before long, you will notice your work becoming stronger and more dynamic.

THE TEXTILE ARTIST'S DESIGN PROCESS

There are distinct stages to the creative process:

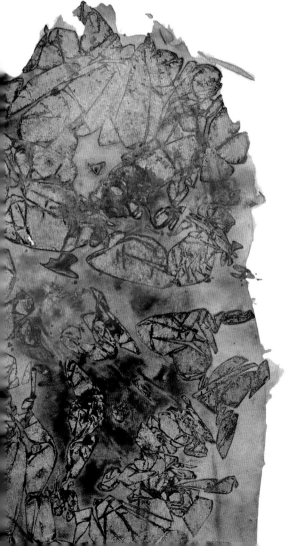

• **Think** This is the important first step. During this phase you find inspirational ideas and concepts – the thoughts and emotions you bring to a subject – and it is these that fuel the development of your design.

• **Look** Next comes observation, sketchbook work, photography, researching your theme, experimenting with collage in fabric and paper, considering styles of design, choosing colours, deciding on types of fabrics and stitches you wish to use and addressing the size and scale of your piece. For me, this is when composition, photography and art begin to merge with fabric and stitch. This is the phase in which a working plan is developed as these explorations become the early design of your piece.

• **Design** During this phase you compose the structure of the piece – the way in which different elements will come together to express your theme with impact – and make final decisions about construction and size.

• **Make** Once your design is chosen, this is the time to explore creative surfaces, choose and create fabrics (using dyes, paints, stamp effects, screen printing or other techniques) and practise the stitch techniques to be used. Your stitched textile piece can be developed through this staged process, or sometimes the 'making' stage can be more spontaneous, drawing both from your research and your emotions.

Above: **Thameside: St. Pauls** (Sandra Meech, UK). Collage from painted and printed photo images. Left: Crinkle effects with dilute acrylic and clingfilm to mimic water.

Starting with questions

Questions are always a good starting point in any creative process. Begin by considering some important questions about the feelings and concepts behind your work, and where you would like to begin.

How do you come up with a design and follow it through?

An initial theme is the starting point. From here, your research will help you discover the elements you will use in your design. A composition can be based on many elements – shapes, contrasting or harmonious values, textures, patterns, stripes, blocks, high/low horizon – or just on colour. Design is the pulling together of the different ingredients and ideas (into a composition) to translate to the viewer information, a vision, a concept or an emotion through fabric and stitch. Textile artists often choose to develop their theme in a series, based on a similar design style. Their work will be cohesive and suitable for a gallery setting, but will still allow for variation.

Is design planned or spontaneous – or a bit of both?

However realistic, interpretive, abstract, expressive or random the final work appears, the majority of artists and designers usually have a plan. This could be the decision to use a restricted colour palette to evoke a particular emotion, or to work consistently with realism (a landscape for example) to create an abstract.

When a theme is decided upon, the journey can become straightforward as you move on to exploring colour and surface techniques with materials appropriate to your chosen subject. We all work in different ways – some make small sketches to begin, or use paper collages to explore ideas. Others develop a design by cropping and isolating photographs, either on a computer or by hand, to prompt the discovery of a dynamic composition. Preparation is key to a good beginning, as it keeps you focused and gives you confidence in your idea and design process.

TEN VITAL DESIGN CONSIDERATIONS

1 Find an inspired theme

Find an idea or inspiration that will take you further than you thought possible, and your finished design will evoke a sense of your inspiration. Using a focused subject (for example, 'the lily') tends to be more useful than a large, less definitive and more generic one (such as 'flowers').

In my teaching of textile design, I ask students to share the personal themes they have brought to the class – subjects that are close to their hearts that they might like to explore in more depth. I am constantly amazed by how diverse these themes are – from realism in the landscape to more conceptual themes, such as ecology, politics, health and social issues or the economy. Everyone identifies with their own sense of place – in their landscape, culture or family.

Colour in all its forms has plenty of emotional appeal, and can be the main inspiration in a chosen subject.

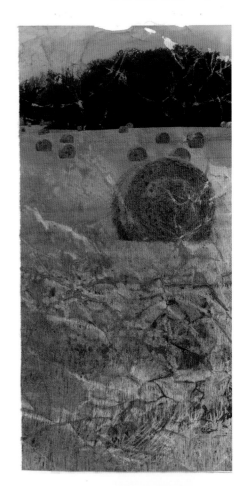

Top: **Bales of Hay**. Made from painted and scrunched colour copies. Above: **A Building**. Composition of painted papers to show windows and reflections. Both images by Sandra Meech, UK.

Below: **La Serenissima** (Jacky Russell, UK) (detail shown far right) explores the textural, fragile and aesthetic quality of decayed architecture, using mixed media to great effect in this dramatic composition.

Establish a theme

Make a list of all the things that you are inspired by or are passionate about, and ideas you keep returning to unconsciously. Go through your photographs – this might reveal a subject or detail that you keep coming back to that is worth exploring.

If you are stuck for ideas on where to look for a theme, consider any of the following:
- **Travels** – colour, textures, the architecture and history of a place. This theme might include water and reflections, textiles, colours, people and traditions. Exotic places offer fascinating subject matter – the colours of spices, markets, textiles and fashions.
- **Home environment**– the farm, the garden, the village near home, patterns from city maps.
- **Pastimes** – trekking, walking, footpaths, maps, music.
- **Cultural pursuits** – music, poetry, drama, ballet, costume, aspects of fashion.
- **Memories** – favourite places, beaches, forest walks, family history (old photographs, stories and letters from the war, for example).
- **Aspects of nature** – ferns, flowers, birds, rock, textures, colour in the seasons.
- **Emotions** – dreams, fantasy, loss, happiness, anxiety and fear.
- **Concepts** – light/dark, smooth/rough, political, economic, global warming, destruction, freedom, breaking down, rust, looking through windows or doors, etc.
- **Textures** (often from nature) – bark, rock, moss, lichen, fish scales, rust.
- **Repeat patterns** – spirals, arches, decorative symbols derived from nature or man-made.

Research your theme

Collecting information on your chosen subject can lots of fun. Photographs you have taken can be a great source of details, textures and colours, especially since these elements have already inspired you enough to take the photographs in the first place. If you keep a diary

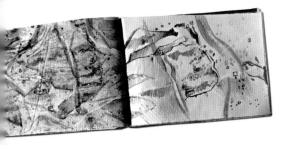

Left: Photos of distressed surfaces and arches in architecture could inspire ideas in a sketchbook. (Sandra Meech, UK)

of events, travels, information you have discovered, and thoughts that occur to you, dip into this to locate anything that is related to your theme. In the same way, keeping a sketchbook is invaluable for recording ideas that can be incorporated into your designs. Research your theme by visiting the library, searching the Internet, or flicking through magazines – old copies of *National Geographic* can provide a wealth of images and knowledge. Bigger issues to do with ecology and nature, politics and social issues can also be linked to your theme, giving it greater depth.

Consolidate your research with a mindmap

Creating a mindmap might be the best way to consolidate and organise your ideas. Before decisions are made about fabric surfaces and stitch, this tool can help you to focus on your subject. Both direct and lateral thinking can reveal a web of ideas, as well as another view or side of your subject that you did not at first consider – all from just a few scribbles on paper. The wonderful thing about mindmaps is that they can be done anywhere, whenever the inspiration takes you. Ensure during the exercise that you are thinking about fabric choices (sheers, heavy or thin, matte or shiny), surface painting or design (monoprinting, screen printing) or how piecing or applied surfaces could enhance the work in addition to the use of stitch.

▶ *To create a mindmap, place your theme centrally on a sheet of paper and draw five to eight tangents from the main subject to explore further. Label these with concepts and ideas associated with your theme. They can be inspired by colour, history, shape or form, interaction with nature, humanity, myth, the seasons, textures, ecological issues, personal emotions and fabric choices. Allow sub-topics to arise to extend your ideas further. Feel free to link different areas, making fresh associations.*

Above: A 'Meltdown' visual mindmap suggests colour, design and conceptual ideas for future work. Clockwise from the top, it includes images of landscapes, melting ice and industrial scenes, some in fabric. It uses copper to represent heat, and, ends with images of how climate change is affecting people and animals in the Arctic.

15

2 Communicate strong ideas

Evidence of a concept or deeper theme can help to make any textile work more dynamic. When there has been thoughtful research, and the many avenues on a subject have been explored, the work will reflect a more consolidated interpretation. Whether a textile is based on a realistic, stylized, abstract, expressive or textural theme, it will be stronger if there is a strong idea behind it.

3 Absorb the principles of design

The lucky few who have a natural sense of good design and balance may leap forwards by several stages to produce strong dynamic compositions, sometimes not even knowing how. But, in order to understand or critique what we have done or recognize design errors, it is important to understand some basic rules. (The principles of design as seen in stitched textiles are explored in chapter 4.)

4 Develop your style

This doesn't come easily (consider how fine artists work for years to develop a personal style), but is worth aspiring to. Developing your own visual style allows you to create pieces of work that speak with one visual focus, in which all the parts of the piece communicate with each other. Keeping your design approach simple might become an identifying signature in itself, as can having a strong point of focus. Be consistent with a 'look' over several pieces of work – people will soon recognize it as a style. The presence of a strong theme or concept in the work will also identify a personal 'style' when viewed with other work.

Opposite: **Gary** (Carole Waller, UK). Transfer print with disperse dyes on a polyester fabric. The glass panels give the illusion of depth, the silhouette a focus, and the border a frame. Below: **Black Water** #5 and **Black Water** #1 (bottom) (both Judy Hooworth, Australia) are part of a dynamic series of textile pieces that show the movement of light on water and the patterns of wind and rain. The compositions are simple but there are many areas to sustain interest.

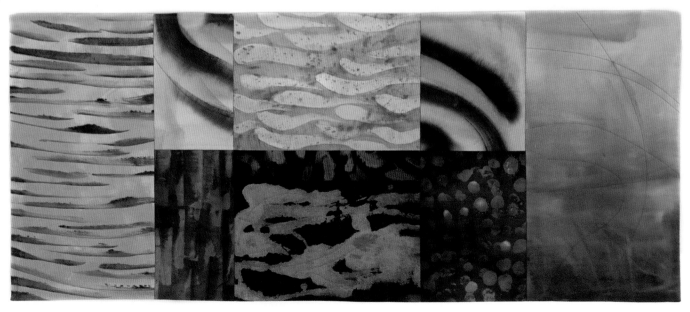

5 Create a dynamic focus

A dynamic design draws the viewer into your work. The strong use of shape, image or colour captures the viewer's interest initially, and then their eye will be led across the rest of the surface.

The concept of the golden section rectangle (see page 35) is one of the most valuable tools for composition. This can help you to establish a centre of interest in your work, and can enable the quilter or embroiderer (who may have learnt her craft through the balance and symmetry of the bed quilt or bordered central motif) to create dynamic compositions.

When it comes to focal points, don't play it safe. Keep the viewer moving around the surface – static design can be dull and symmetry just as boring. In looking at abstraction on pages 96–103, we will see the use of focal points taken to extremes.

6 Use colour and surface techniques wisely

Colour carries with it not only a pure and simple reflection of the subject but also psychological and emotional resonances. The choice of colour can make or break the success of a stitched-textile piece. Choose colours that are right, not those that are expected. Take chances once in a while. (The use of colour will be covered in more depth on pages 74–77.)

When it comes to surface techniques and embellishment, bear in mind that too much time spent on the latest products and techniques can be counterproductive. Be careful not to introduce too many different techniques, piecing methods or surface art cloth techniques, as it can make work look very uneven and unresolved.

7 Use positive and negative space

Empty space, be it dark or light, allows the viewer's attention to be drawn to other elements of the composition. Therefore, although it can be neutral, the negative space is as important as the busy filled part because it provides a place for the eye to rest. For example, graphic designers use empty space in the layout of magazine pages to enable the reader to focus on an important headline or photograph. This principle can be applied with great effect in wall-hung stitched textiles as well.

Above: **Icebreak, Meltdown IV** (Sandra Meech, UK). This piece, at almost 2m (6ft) wide, represents the constant break-up of ice in the polar regions. Detail shown above right. Far left: **Tate Wall 1** (Sandra Meech, UK). Reflections of city buildings. Left: Photograph of a construction site (Sandra Meech, UK)– a perfect rectangular viewing area complete with wire grid. Right (middle): **Meltdown 1** (Sandra Meech, UK). From a series of textile pieces each 1m (3ft) square, based on melting ice, inspired by images in Iceland. Right: A graphic simplification of the positive and negative spaces in Meltdown 1.

8 Simplifying – less is more

When there is just too much information in a piece of work (too many surface techniques or over-embellishment) it is difficult for the viewer to see what you want them to focus on. Consider how much media consumer information we are constantly exposed to, and how we strive for a bit of calm in our lives. A busy surface can confuse the message of the piece as well as the viewer, while restrained sections of texture and embellishment, well placed on the surface, can create a much more dramatic result than huge swathes of texture.

Cropping or isolating a section of a photo can help to simplify it, and will also make it more dramatic – you will see many occasions throughout this book when we use this technique to pare down a subject/technique/pattern to the essentials for dramatic effect.

Above: **Shadows – were we there?** (Fenella Davies, UK) One of a series of abstract textile compositions that have an elusive quality, as muted colours and shapes dissolve back and forth across the surface.
Opposite: **Arctic Snow** (Sandra Meech, UK). A small textile piece that illustrates the colours of spring snow. Machine stitch forms a pattern across the simply pieced surface.

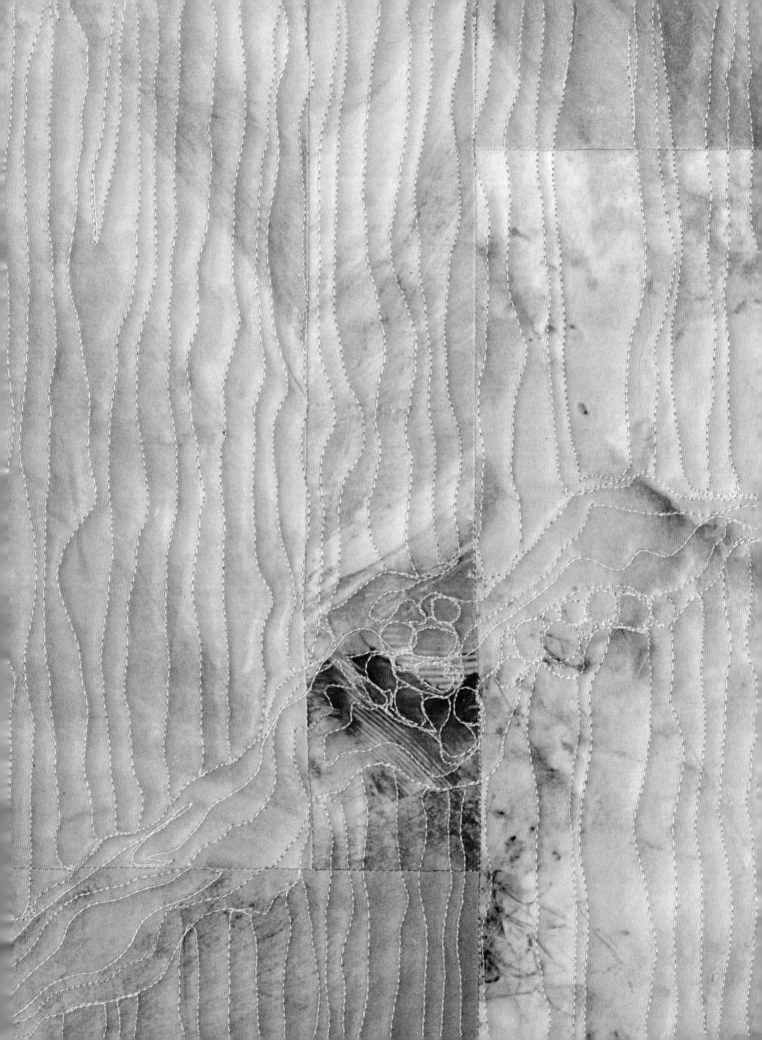

9 Be original

This is easier said than done. The more exposure you have to stitched-textile disciplines, or design in general, the more you will absorb ideas and influences, be it consciously or subconsciously. Fine artists have for generations been influenced by each other's work while striving to develop a recognizable and individual style of their own. It is probably impossible to prevent elements from pieces of work you have been inspired by from finding their way into the work you do, but if you develop your own personal themes, and explore colour and texture independently, there is no reason why you should not be influenced by other sources, as you will still be creating original pieces of work. Do your own thing, be independent, find your own creative voice and try not to be derivative. If you find you are only learning someone else's style or technique, it might be helpful to limit the number of workshops you take.

10 Trust your own judgement

Design is based on a series of visual decisions that become easier to make the more you practise making them. There will be choices to make and perhaps a few different compositions to try but, often, the first design idea will just feel right, and this is the one to choose. Save the other designs for future work in a series. Make firm decisions. If you are going for something strong and powerful, follow it through. You may practise several compositions on a smaller scale at first, but one design will stand out.

Use a design wall (see page 24) and live with a composition for a while. Look at it regularly, turn it upside down, view a mirror image of it or look at it through the camera lens. Fresh ways of looking at your work will enable you to see any design flaws that you previously missed.

Far left: **Orange Flower Pod 2** (Gordana Brelih, Canada). Left: **Medusa and Cerberus** (Sam Morris, UK). Mythology mixe[d] with dark humour is the focus for t[he] very original cushion.

Developing intuition

Some people have an intuitive ability to compose different elements in an interesting way. Understanding and reviewing the tried-and-tested compositional tools available to artists will make design decisions easier to make. What is practised enough times becomes intuitive – as when playing a musical instrument.

Above: **The First Ladies Getting Home**
(Janet Bolton, UK) tells a story of fields, fences, pathways and sheep with homespun fabrics in a shaped composition.

23

DESIGN ESSENTIALS

A design wall

Having a design wall is vital – and it doesn't have to be large. This is the place to hang artwork, photographs, paper collage, fabrics, and anything you find inspiring. It can also be used as a blank canvas on which to test out your compositions on a large scale, giving you the opportunity to analyze areas of interest, movement and depth across the surface, light and shade and scale and proportion, and to spot design flaws. A design wall can give you a good idea of how your work might hang in a gallery, and it provides a space where you can take photographs of your work at different stages of development.

A camera

Throughout this book, there will be many instances in which a subject or theme is directly inspired by a photograph. Using a digital camera, computer, scanner and printer can become an important starting point for the stitched-textile artist. These tools are not meant to replace drawing, painting or sketching, or undermine what can be achieved with hand or machine stitch, but they can provide you with an immediate way of looking and seeing the potential in your ideas.

Taking photographs enables you to study detail, texture and colour in your subject immediately. Any image can be used directly on cloth or abstracted to become the source of a design, so when you shoot a subject, ensure you take pictures of its details, too. They can reveal textures and even surprising colours you may not have noticed when looking at the subject as a whole.

As you take photographs, you also get an excellent opportunity to put the principles of good composition into practice. Fine artists working in the landscape will often use their thumb and forefinger or a card viewfinder to isolate a focal point. You can use your camera's viewfinder in the same way, using the rule of thirds to establish a centre of interest. Some cameras have an inbuilt grid which divides up the viewfinder according to the rule of thirds.

Downloading photos onto the computer allows you to see your images in many different ways. For instance, a picture can be cropped for a more abstract view. Also, colour photos can be converted to black and white, or lightened and contrasted to enhance line and shape. Painting black-and-white images can provide ideas to use in future collage compositions. Try some of the following exercises:

▶ *Take one image and crop it in many different ways. Try using angled squares or rectangles for interest.*
▶ *Create a series of lightened and high-contrast black-and-white images from colour pictures, then look at them to spot details you might have missed in colour. Now consider how the details you have noticed might inform stitched line and collaged fabric shapes.*
▶ *Make colour photocopies of your prints, some of which you should enlarge. Cut them up and re-assemble the pieces to make a pleasing photo-collage composition.*

Left, top to bottom: A collection of photos from the Dordogne, France, with abstract details. An image of an old bicycle in colour and black and white is then enlarged for an interesting simple composition. Right: **Flood** (Sandra Meech, UK). A photo and painted paper collage based on tidal flow at West Bay, Dorset.

Art materials

Before you begin work on any of the exercises in this book, you will need to gather a set of art materials. Many of the exercises require some drawing, painting, sketching and collage, so it is best to have everything to hand.

You will need:

- Your own photographs, enlarged to A4 size and photocopied in colour and black and white
- A black felt tip and thick and thin permanent pens, and a range of soft pencils
- A cutting board, knife and paper scissors
- A pad of good sketching paper, and some tracing paper
- Coloured pencils, oil pastels, watercolour paints or Brusho (watercolour dyes), and acrylic paint in a range of colours, including white
- Acetate sheets (A4 size)
- A glue stick and PVA glue
- A range of coloured fabrics for colour exercises – hand-dyed, Bali and batik styles work well. Also useful are any black and white and neutral fabrics and fabrics with large, medium and small prints
- Some thin wadding (batting) and backing fabrics, for stitch design exercises
- A sewing machine and range of threads
- Magazines, which are good for layout and composition ideas or to cut and tear for colour and texture collage examples. *National Geographic* is great for this purpose, as are interior design, travel, home and gardening magazines. Newspapers that include interesting headlines could also be painted.

Use these materials experimentally to help you develop your ideas. Throughout the book, I suggest ways in which to create marks and textures that could suggest interesting patterns and surfaces.

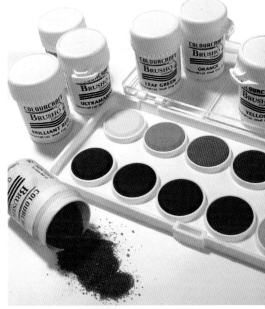

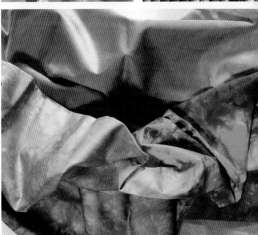

Above, from top: Brusho powder dye paints and a Koh-i-Noor paint palette; threads, coloured pencils and sumptuous dyed fabric (Heidi Stoll-Weber, Germany); a sketchbook is always close at hand.

Creating mixed-media surfaces for design exercises

Creating surfaces in paper and on cloth can be an interesting and fruitful exercise. Use the art materials you have gathered to create painted, stamped and printed textures that, combined with resists on textured paper and fabric, will provide materials for future design exercises. Imagery in the form of colour and black-and-white copies can also be used to explore new approaches to composition. Throughout this book we will work on compositions on a small scale and, later, consider how designs could be enlarged. Some will be independent collages and others will be kept in a bound sketchbook.

Photocopies

Prepare sets of photocopies, each based on a theme you would like to develop. Enlarge images and details to full size in colour to fill the page, and make several black-and-white copies of each. When preparing black-and-white copies on the computer, lighten them and increase the contrast so blacks are strong and the image has fewer halftone greys. Printing with a laser printer will give you the best results.

Acrylic paint

- Student-quality acrylic tube paints used directly on thin white cotton can create some interesting colourful surfaces in theme colours. Ensure you layer two to three pieces of cloth together. Start by working on fat-quarter size pieces. Acrylic dyes can also be applied onto cotton with a brush to give the cotton a smooth and soft look.
- Black and white commercial cotton can also be painted on with acrylic paints to create some interesting effects.
- Textured wallpaper can be used as a stamp, which could provide an interesting starting point for textural ideas. Consider creating two or three colourways to begin with, perhaps in warm-colour and cool-colour combinations.
- A palette-knife painting using acrylic paints on a black-and-white photocopy can be good to use for collage (see page 100).
- Dilute acrylic paints on Bondaweb (painted in the direction of the grain) will produce a linear texture, or it can be scrunched up. Both produce different effects when left to dry for 24 hours, then ironed face-down onto cotton.
- Acrylic or screen-printing inks can be rolled onto scrunched-up and flattened foil, which then acts as a stamp to use on white cloth to produce an interesting texture.

Above left: a variety of fabric surfaces including commercial cottons, plain and painted cloth, transfer-dyed images on interfacing, screen printing on cloth and stamp effects from vinyl wallpaper. Left: Crinkle effects made with dilute acrylic paint applied to the glue side of Bondaweb, scrunched, dried then ironed onto white cotton.

Dyes and watercolours

- There are some simple dyeing methods that are great for experimentation. Easy-to-apply dye/paint (such as Deka silk paints) can be applied to silk or cotton and heat-set when dry. Acrylic inks can also be used to dye fabrics. Bringing together some small squares of dyed fabrics will be handy for design and collage work.
- Try painting black-and-white photocopies with Brusho or Procion dyes to produce a wonderful source of textured coloured papers for collage.

Transfer-dye techniques

- Disperse transfer dyes can be mixed and painted onto thin white paper, then ironed onto Vilene interfacing or other non-woven style materials. You can add marks to the paper with wax resist before painting (a candle or white wax crayon works well) to create some interesting patterns. These types of small sample fabrics you create could be mixed with paper for small collage exercises. The used painted paper (after all the transfer dye has been ironed off) is also wonderful to use for collage exercises.
- Transfer dyes also work well on commercial black-and-white quilting cotton when the sizing has been left in.

Printing techniques

Dyed fabrics are used for some of the exercises in this book. If you have access to the equipment necessary for the following printing techniques, give them a try to produce your sample fabrics – experimentation can produce very interesting results.

- Screen printing. With every theme you are developing ideas for, find a drawing or photograph that could be screen printed for an interesting effect. There are services available online that can provide a thermofax screen ready for use.
- Monoprinting. This technique is fun and easy to try. It could provide some interesting marks on cloth and paper that you can use for the exercises throughout this book.
- Stamps, handmade or commercial, can be used to create interesting additions to surfaces. Stamps are easy to make (you can use craft-foam shapes mounted onto foam board), and can be used with screen-printing inks rolled onto them. Begin by using small stamps.

However, you might well find very interesting dyed patterns in your stash of coloured fabrics. As previously mentioned, Bali- and batik-style fabrics will work very well with many of the exercises to come.

Above, from top: Photocopies arranged in an abstract composition; photocopy coloured with dilute Brusho; pattern created by drawing on cloth that was later transfer-dyed; an image drawn and painted directly onto T-shirt transfer paper, then ironed onto white cotton fabric. Left: This fabric was created by drawing with permanent pens onto polyester-sateen fabric.

Tools and materials

- A 23cm × 30cm (9in × 12in), A4-size white or cream sketching-paper pad, with paper of at least 120gsm in weight, containing at least 20 sheets
- Brusho paints, watercolours, or Procion dyes
- At least five colour photographs on a personal theme; three of a whole image and two of a detail/texture. Make two matte A4 colour photocopies of each of these; create a black-and-white image of each colour photo on your computer (lighten and contrast them) and print at least four copies of each. We now have ten colour copies and at least 20 black-and-white.
- Five sheets of A4 tracing paper or thin parchment
- A craft knife, a metal-edged ruler, a cutting board, pen or pencil, elastic bands, paper scissors, a chenille or binding needle
- Waxed linen binding thread and binding needle
- Bone folder and ruler
- Stranded cotton or embroidery floss in several colours that are related to your theme
- A glue stick and beads

MAKING A BOUND SKETCHBOOK

Every artist needs a sketchbook in which to collect ideas and inspirations when developing design ideas for new work. For this design class, we will paint papers and bind them together to create a sketchbook for future reference.

Painting and scoring

- Paint at least 20 pages of the sketchbook quickly, one after the other, filling the whole page. Remove them from the sketchpad and allow to dry.
- Paint at least ten of the black-and-white photocopies and allow to dry.
- When both sets of painted pages are dry, tear into two long pieces lengthwise.
- Score and tear at least four sheets of A4 tracing paper.

Making and binding signatures

A 'signature' in a book is a set of pages that are all folded in half together, in a bundle. Books are made up of groups of signatures bound together. There will be eight signatures in this book, each using five sheets of paper. These will include two painted sketchbook papers – one on the outside and one on the inside of the signature, one colour copy, one black-and-white copy and a layer of tracing paper. If your sketchbook paper is thin, then more coloured paper can be included in an individual signature.

- For each signature, stack up your five pieces of paper and fold them down the middle. Create eight of these signatures.
- Using a separate marked paper for reference, make six evenly spaced marks along the spine of each signature with a pen or pencil. Make holes where you have marked the spines on the outside cover of each signature, using the binding needle. Now stack the signatures, ready for binding, and hold them together with elastic bands to keep them aligned.
- Thread about 40cm (16in) of waxed linen thread onto the binding needle. Now thread through each of the corresponding holes in each signature, in the order indicated in the illustration below left. Ensure you leave 7.5cm (3in) of thread spare at the end. Stitch through the spine and knot in the middle as illustrated (below, middle).
- With stranded cotton (no longer than 46cm [18in]), knot to secure in the centre section, leaving 7.5cm (3in), and weave through the linen thread back and forth. Consider changing the colour if you wish. Knot the stranded cotton at the end (see illustration below right).
- The covers can be thickened by gluing on extra paper, coloured image card or fabric if you would like, and embellished with beads.

Consider some of the compositional exercises on the next page using your own reference. These are only suggestions – your own pages will look different.

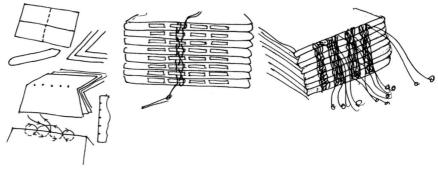

High horizon/Low horizon is a good composition to begin with. Stick simple shapes made from torn, painted or printed photocopies onto some of the painted pages.

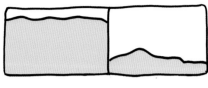

Curves Use a simple coloured spread as a background. Cut several curves at the same time through two or three different papers and arrange as shown above.

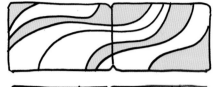

Strips and stripes can be made up of varied widths of torn reference material. This composition gives movement across the page. Consider the placement of any spot colour.

Adding line The detail in colour or black-and-white reference images can be extended across the page as lines. This is good practice for drawing and can inspire stitch.

Tracing-paper pages can be placed next to photo details or line drawings. The effects on the opposite page are interesting and could suggest the use of sheer fabrics for transparency in a textile piece.

Blocks Cut out three rectangles from a colour-copy reference the size of one page and glue onto the opposite page. Fill in detail with line, oil pastels or coloured pencils.

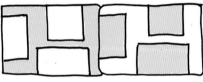

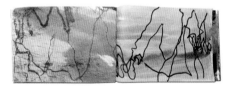

Marks could include repeat detail from a natural reference, or a symbol that refers directly to a particular theme. Enlarge, reduce or overlap the marks to create pattern.

Squares and rectangles can also provide an interesting composition across the page. Remember to extend the information onto the painted background. Do you see a new textile piece emerging?

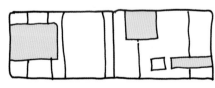

Torn pages can create dimensional interest. Use a series of four or five different-coloured page spreads or coloured and black-and-white photo pages with plain painted pages. Consider colour as interest moves across the page spread.

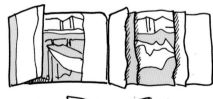

Cut-out shapes on torn pages could suggest a layered or perhaps suspended textile piece.

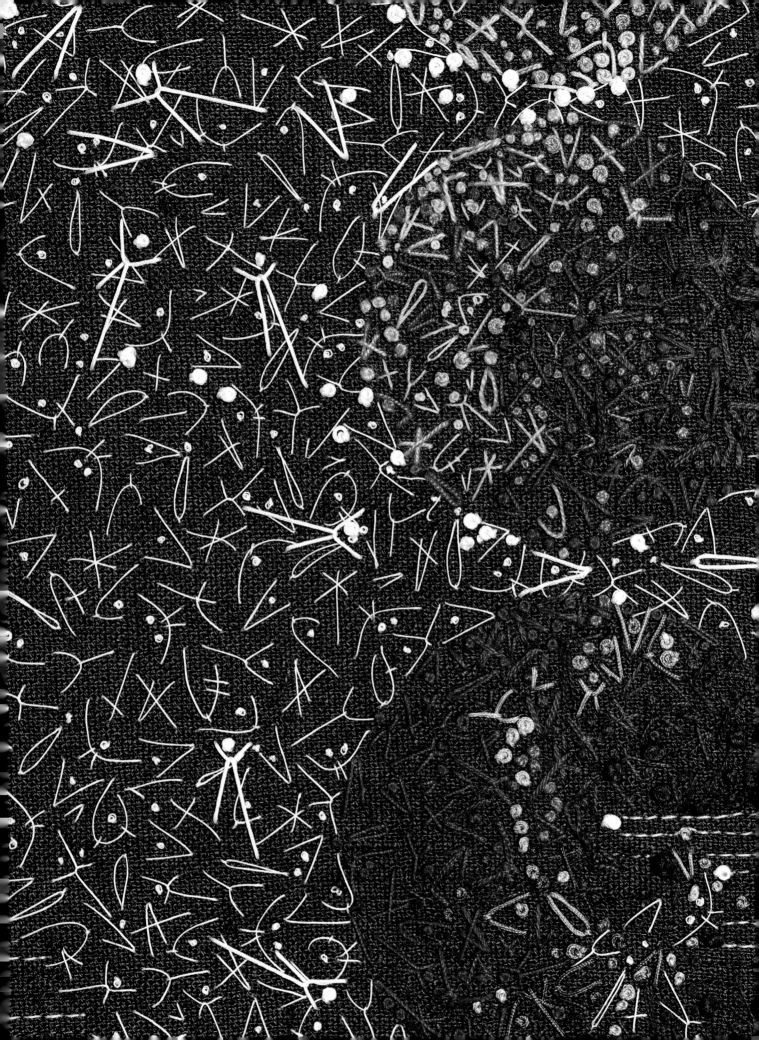

DESIGN STYLES

There is a world of design sources out there, which could strongly influence the way forward in developing your theme. Design influences are everywhere, in all disciplines from window dressing in a department store to furnishing fabrics made with a nod to the latest trends and patterns. Historic textiles, architecture old and new, or a poster advertisement, billboard or magazine layout could spark a new idea.

As design becomes a natural part of our lives, we can learn to appreciate it more fully, and our textiles will be richer for it. Considering the wealth of design sources available to us, it is no wonder it is hard to choose what to look at first, and that it may take some time just to consolidate ideas, collect research materials and find graphic shapes and images to inspire us before we actually get started on a piece of work.

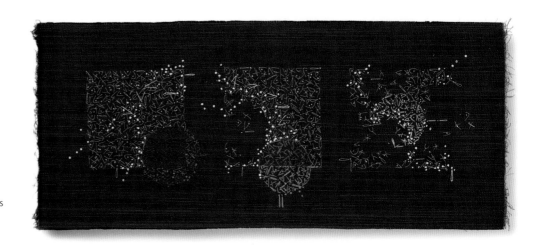

Left: **Evolution 1** (detail) (Maggie Barber, UK). Full piece shown on page 68). Right: **Evolution 4** (Maggie Barber, UK). Extraordinary depth of stitch marks and subtle use of colour is demonstrated in this series of work.

dark rust health Venice bark
spirals memories colours music
light trees happiness culture trekking
family contrasts embroidery spice windows
travels markets footpaths garden people
history fantasy refections seaside
beaches India themes flowers texture
Arctic fabrics arches maps textiles

NATURE'S DESIGN

We can appreciate our natural environment from an early age – butterflies, sunflowers and seashells are not only beautiful, but perfectly designed. We can enjoy changing colour, pattern, texture, and detail everywhere in the landscape. Your camera can be an important tool for documenting what you see in nature. Use natural light – the dark and cloudy, rainy, or misty day, or bright sunshine with its high contrasts – to add further interest to your photographs as you record what you see to use later.

Images from nature have dominated themes in stitched textiles and other art forms for hundreds of years. In ancient Egypt, stylized flowers in repetitive patterns of red, yellow and blue were evident on bowls and murals. Dutch damask wall panels, tapestries, floral embroidery, chintz and silks from the Far East, flower fabrics and pattern for wallpaper and textiles continue to influence textile design. Japanese design has traditionally expressed natural themes, and it has been a strong influence in the worlds of fine art and graphic design. Nature's influence on Western design is also evident – consider the fabric and wallpaper designs of William Morris, or the flower-power fashion designs popular in the 1970s, or even more recently as retro designs.

To use nature as a source of ideas, consider the following:

▶ *Create a collection of torn page references from magazines that show how nature has influenced design both past and present.*
▶ *Bring together a collection of your own photographs from nature – flowers, birds, butterflies, trees or rock formations. Include whole subjects and details from your subjects. Print 13cm × 18cm (5in × 7in) glossy images for drawing and sketching reference. Make several enlarged photocopies for future design collages.*
▶ *Take one image of a natural object, crop and enlarge it several times on the computer to see how abstract it could become. This could inspire a future design.*
▶ *Write a full page about an aspect of nature – a memory, an experience or feelings about something you have seen.*
▶ *Select a picture that shows an example of a historical textile style based on nature, enlarge it to abstract and make it your own (your own surfaces, images and colours).*

Left, from top: Photo inspirations from nature; a William Morris fabric design, plus a detail from it that has been digitally manipulated with inverted colour in Photoshop Elements to give an abstract effect.

Left: Cropping and enlarging a detail of a butterfly's wing to make it more abstract, and perhaps adding some words about the subject, could become part of a new design.

Above: **Butterland** (Elizabeth Brimelow, UK). This depiction of fields in the Pennines is an excellent example of a large, dynamic, stylized composition that includes realistic detail.

The Fibonacci sequence

Fibonacci, a thirteenth-century mathematician, arrived at a sequence of numbers in which each number is the sum of the previous two: $0+1=1$; $1+1=2$; $1+2=3$; $2+3=5$; $3+5=8$; $5+8=13$; $8+13=21$. and so on. This pattern is found everywhere in nature – in the swirl of a conch shell, the nodules on a pine cone or the seeds in the centre of a sunflower – and has been used in art, architecture and textiles through the centuries. Consider how the patterns in African and other historic border design has derived from the proportions in the Fibonacci sequence. The golden section rectangle (shown right) is based on this number sequence, and you can immediately see where the center of interest is located. If you base the proportions in your textile work on any part of the series, it will always 'look right'.

The rule of thirds

The rule of thirds has long been used by photographers and artists as a basic compositional tool, and it is just as important to textile artists. According to this design rule, when an area is broken into thirds both horizontally and vertically (by two horizontal lines and two vertical lines), the area where two of the lines intersect creates a centre of interest. Once chosen, this dominant area can be identified in a number of ways, with colour, shape, directional lines or texture, to bring the viewer into the overall surface design of the piece. Often, one primary centre of interest is enough, but frequently a secondary, smaller focal point can help to balance the design, and this can be placed on the point where two of the lines intersect at the opposite corner to the main focal point. It is worth noting that if there is a point of interest where all the lines intersect, the focus becomes central to the whole design and it becomes symmetrical.

HINT Remember – never make any two intervals the same. An 'interval' in this case refers not only to an area or space, but to shape, colour, texture or tonal value – any of the elements in your composition.

Opposite: **Morston: Masts and Shrouds** (top) and **Morston: Curlew** (bottom) (Debbie Lyddon, UK). Both pieces, from a series based on the Norfolk coast, are strong compositions. Each piece in the series is named after a sound and the place in which it was heard. In Morston: Curlew, the placement of a focal point (the sun or moon shape on the top left) is balanced by the square shape in the bottom right of the composition.

Right, from top to bottom: The Fibonacci spiral overlaid on a photo taken at Stonehenge. The person in red has become the focal point or centre of interest; the perfect spiral, found in ammonites, shells, sunflowers, a flower head or pine cone; the proportions of Leonardo Da Vinci's Vetruvian Man are based on the golden section rectangle; a photograph of flowers, with the red focal point for interest; the pattern in which leaves grow can also be seen in a sunflower head. Look closely and a radiating pattern can be seen.

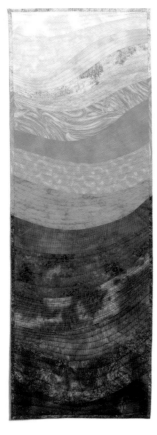

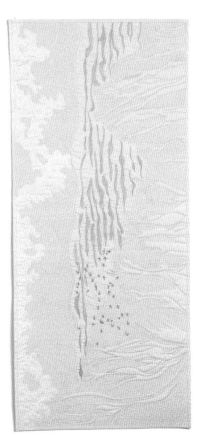

Landscape

A landscape that inspires you is a wonderful starting point for expressing yourself creatively. Many compositions in art and stitched textiles have their starting point in a landscape. The Impressionists responded to colour and light in the landscape expressively. Rivers flow and curve in the landscape, forests and lakes come and go, salt lakes form, icebergs melt, sand beaches shift… all this happens naturally. An aerial view can illustrate both the wild, untouched landscape as well as the pattern of Man's organisation. Managed agricultural fields, dark furrows in rich soil, rows of new green growth or dead stalks can be a constant source of design possibilities.

Above: **Breakers** (Sheena Norquay, Scotland). Contrast and movement combine with colour and stitch in this dynamic series. Left: **New England Seashore** (photograph: Sandra Meech, UK). Below: **Truro to Nauset Light** (Dawn Thorne, UK). A weathered storm fence on a stretch of beach in Cape Cod. Opposite: **Scatter 1** (Dawn Thorne, UK) Shadows form in dimension in this innovative work based on nature.

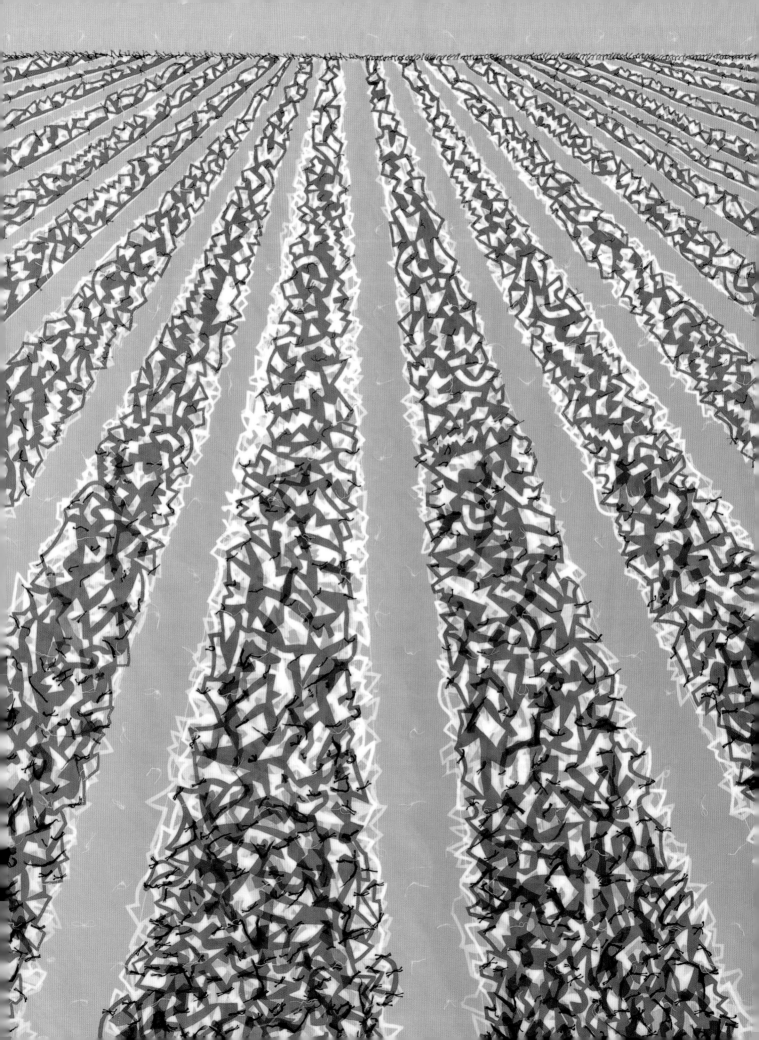

▶ *Collect images to illustrate Man's organization of nature – rows of corn or other crops and vineyards offer great inspiration in terms of colour and texture. Use your own photographs, or gather research material. What patterns can you detect?*

The stylized landscape is a contemporary approach to landscape painting. Hills and valleys lend themselves well to this style. Perspective can be flattened to produce graphic shapes, and this style translates well in textiles and art quilts. Consider David Hockney's exploration of the California hills over wide panels full of movement and colour.

▶ *Stylize a landscape from a photograph, perhaps using extremes of colour for effect. Consider how this design might become a stitched textile. See page 103 for more about abstracts and stylizing an image.*

Opposite: **Feltwell Furrows** (Elizabeth Brimelow, UK). This transparent, double-sided silk quilt, with its high-horizon composition, gives an 'overground/underground' view of a winter scene. Right: This digitally enhanced image from a hilltop photo in Belves, France could inspire a stylized contemporary quilt.

Above: **Spanish Serenade** (Carol Naylor, UK) is inspired by the landscape near Castille, Spain. Intense machine stitch gives a luminous feel across the whole surface.

39

Opposite: **Structured** (Hannah Payne, UK).
A shipyard and industry on the Isle of
Sheppey inspired digital imagery on silk.
Left: **Missed Opportunities** (top) and **The
Threshold** (bottom) (Helen Colling, UK) give
an ethereal feeling in shadow and transparent
imagery in these architectural settings,
encouraging the viewer to study the undefined
details. Below: Photographs of architecture and
industry, old and new (Sandra Meech, UK).

DESIGN BY MAN

Architecture

Buildings of one form or another have been a major part of the human environment for
centuries. Originally simply practical in nature, buildings have evolved to fulfil many purposes
and incorporate various decorative styles, and inspire many people in different ways. Architects
have used the golden section (see page 35) when designing buildings since Ancient Greek times,
and many buildings been elevated into monuments of beauty.

We tend not to notice the familiar as much as the unfamiliar, so we often appreciate buildings
more when we are travelling, as the novelty of the design style of a new country can catch our
interest immediately. This inspiration could be developed into a new body of work – arches,
doorways, alleyways, bridges in Venice, Mediterranean villas or modern skyscrapers can all lead
you in interesting creative directions. Even the familiar can become interesting when you look at
it in a different way. Take a walk with your camera and photograph the architecture around you,
both old and new, whether a town or city, or structures in a rural setting. Consider the reflections
in windows, the textures on distressed door panels, or the forms and patterns found on a
construction site.

▶ *Buildings can conjure up concepts like containment, confinement, freedom and protection.*
Think of some symbols that might depict these four ideas.

The textures found in architectural details can also be inspirational. Focus on grids of wire,
stonework, peeling plaster and paintwork, stone carvings, repeat patterns in railings and gates.
For each photograph you take, there may be countless compositions possible.

experience
shopshopshop
shopshopshop
BURRO DI CACAO
Idratante
shopshopshop
pping shopping shopping
OP SHO
destin

Town planning

Man has established through the centuries planned ways for our societies to develop – consider patterns of feudal European cities, geometric styles of walled towns in France or the cities of North America that are based on a north-south grid. From local maps you can see how towns spread along rivers or are stopped by mountains. Study the patterns and designs in maps. Look at contour lines and any other additional marks in the landscape that could become a stitch or overall quilt design.

▶ *Look at a local map (Ordnance Survey maps are good). Notice the different sizes of the roads, pathways, bridges, borders and contour lines. Look also at the symbols for swamps, ridges and historic monuments. Create a collection of design symbols for your own reference.*

Monuments and sculpture

Monuments, old and new – from stone circles, ancient burial grounds and prehistoric chalk images to modern sculptures found in public places – could conjure design possibilities. The stories behind commemorative statues you find intriguing can be worth investigating, as they may yield sources of inspiration for work in three dimensions. Sculpture parks are accessible to everyone. Sculptures by Henry Moore, Barbara Hepworth, Jacob Epstein, Andy Goldsworthy and Antony Gormley are just a few that are worth investigating. Take photographs and make sketches *in situ*, all the time considering how light and shade changes at different angles.

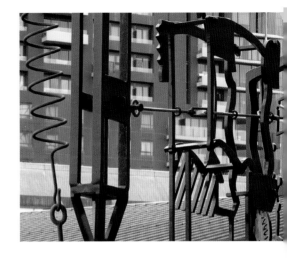

Opposite: **Mall (detail)** (Janet Cairney, UK). Above: Architectural sculpture, Melbourne, Australia. Below, left to right: **Mall**, **Tourists**, **Re-generation** and **Decisions** (Janet Cairney, UK), a dramatic series of fabric-collage illustrations with stitch, showing everyday urban life.

Household objects

'If you want a golden rule that will fit everything, this is it: Have nothing in your houses that you do not know to be useful or believe to be beautiful.' **William Morris**

Furniture was once made for practical purposes only but, over the centuries, its design has developed to the point at which chairs, tables and other types of furniture have become more than just useful things. The Eames Lounge Chair, for example, is a useful and very beautiful object of desire. We can see many of the principles of design at work in these objects and learn from them. Styles of furniture and interior decor vary enormously – some are highly decorative, while others are minimalist. Baroque, Georgian, Victorian and Scandinavian styles, to name just a few, have all influenced the contemporary and abstract art of today. It is also interesting to consider how different materials and industrial methods have impacted on the look and comfort of these household items.

▶ *Look around your home at pieces of furniture, old or new. Look for an interesting detail on a familiar piece of furniture and sketch or photograph this detail.*
▶ *Visit a local auction room and take photographs of interesting objects. Look at your photographs – can you identify any features from which design ideas might evolve?*
▶ *Find a plate in your collection of tableware. Isolate an interesting detail from it. Think about how you can use it abstracted in a piece of work.*

There are many originally domestic objects that can influence your work. Ceramic styles are worth studying for their decoration, design and shape. Stitched textiles have often been influenced by historical objects such as bowls, baskets, caskets, jewellery boxes and vases. Visit museums, such as the Smithsonian in Washington, the Victoria & Albert Museum in London or the Louvre in Paris, to encounter a wealth of design inspiration.

Above left: Stained glass from the V&A Museum, London inspired this quilt using a creative border treatment (Sandra Meech, UK), and a pattern from a William Morris textile rendered in line. Top: **Urbanisation** (Sarahjane Harrison, UK). This refurbished chair includes hand-printed fabric and was inspired by the streets of Liverpool. Above: Antique markets with china and interesting household objects could offer great potential for a theme (photos Sandra Meech, UK).

Left: **Brighton Sea and Downs II** (Wendy Dolan, UK). Maps will always intrigue the viewer and the direction of the stitch adds interest.

45

Textiles

After nature and landscapes, perhaps, textiles form one of the greatest influences in contemporary stitch and other craft disciplines today. The history of the world through civilization can be seen in textiles, in dyed, woven, printed and painted fabrics and skins, embellished with embroidery, beads, mirrors, sequins, tassels and beautiful stitch work. It is through textiles that man has decorated himself and the environment around him, and protected himself from the elements. Skins that were used for protection are still a major material in Inuit communities in northern Canada. Ancient linens from Egyptian times and felt from Mongolia have only survived because of unique climatic circumstances. Most early textiles have not been preserved. From a design point of view we learn from textiles about pattern, construction, styles of making and colour.

Consider an early Coptic pattern and how, by isolating a triangular section of it and rotating and repeating the motif, you can create a modern design. African barkcloth can also become an interesting design inspiration for an abstract piece of textile. Some photo imagery or symbolism, perhaps in the form of a stamped repeat pattern, could be incorporated.

▶ *Borrow a book on the history of textiles from your local library. Learn about the decorative styles of different parts of the world – the Far East, along the Silk Route to India, Victorian design, North American Indian beadwork, Moorish textiles and early North American quilting designs, for instance. Consider how these styles may have influenced more modern works, and which of these styles influences you. How? Why?*
▶ *Consider combining the pattern from a traditional textile with a photographic image. Below I have joined the pattern of an African Kuba cloth textile with an image of the red soil from Australia. A section of this could perhaps inspire an art quilt.*

For more exercises using textiles for design inspiration, see page 80.

Left, from top: Pattern from a 19th-century water jar (Pueblo, New Mexico); strip-woven Kente cloth (West Africa); a design by William Morris; colourful Mola textile (Central America); detail of a 19th-century log-cabin quilt (England). Above and right: African Kuba cloth combined in Photoshop with an image of the Australian outback as an idea for a future quilt.

Above: **Through Lace Walls** (Cas Holmes, UK).
Collected materials from India incorporate stitch and
print. The strips of red contrast with the cool blocks of
blue, creating a balanced but abstract composition.

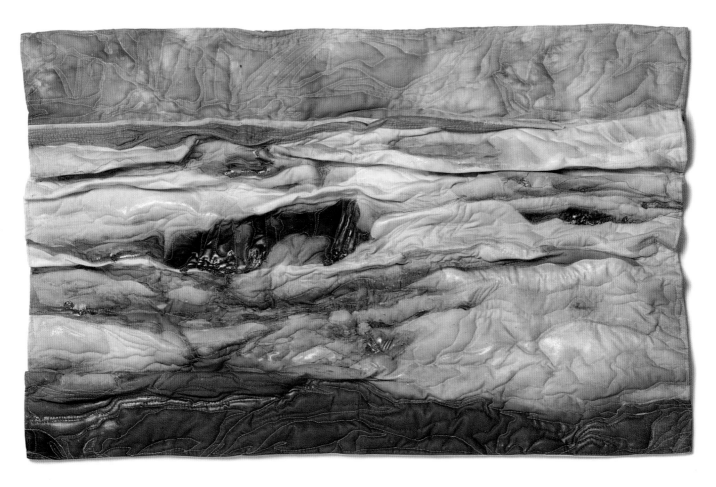

Dimensional textiles

Many contemporary textile artists are directly inspired by sculpture or three-dimensional fine-art objects, in which woven and non-woven fabrics are often mixed with other media such as ceramics, wire, metal and glass. Humorous and quirky artistic creations, such as figures and dolls, can be full of individual personality and textural character that might inspire the stitched-textile artist. Sometimes, two-dimensional work can be displayed off the wall, creating a very modern approach to showing stitched-textile art pieces. In a textile exhibition a variety of dimensional work displayed on plinths or as free-standing installations along with wall-hung work will always interest viewers.

▶ *Build up a collection of 'visuals' showing interesting contemporary three-dimensional textiles.*
▶ *Sketch a design for a textural, dimensional piece of work that uses Wireform. As you develop your idea, consider the rhythm and flow of the piece.*

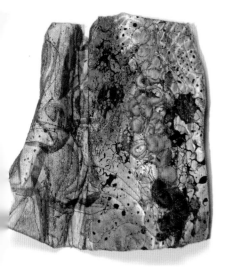

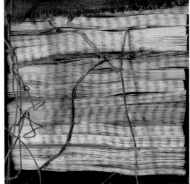

Above: A mixed-media surface was created with painted Bondaweb and transfer dye on cotton, embellished with wool to form a top layer. Next a layer of thin wadding was attached, then a layer of Wireform, and lastly a backing fabric. As the piece is small, the layers were pinned together and machine stitched. Once the stitching was finished, the piece was manipulated for dimension (Sandra Meech, UK).

Left: **Ice Flow 1** (top), **Ice Flow 2** (bottom) (Sandra Meech, UK), part of the 'Meltdown' series. Wireform was used to create dimension with a collage of heat-transferred ice images. The use of positive and negative space implies the landscape.

Right: **Profusion** (Mary Morris, UK) (details shown above). Repeat block shapes always create a strong composition, and the individuality of each block engages the viewer.

Fashion

Throughout history, fashion has been closely aligned with textiles, as most cloth was woven, dyed, painted and decorated for clothing. Clothing fabrics today can include a number of different surface treatments, including discharge dyeing, disperse and indigo dyeing, devoré, batik and resist silk painting, to name a few. Screen-printing methods that include breakdown printing are often transformed into wonderful fashion textiles such as scarves and wraps. Accessories such as jewellery, shoes and bags also make wonderful subjects in stitched textiles.

▶ *Gather reference material by taking photographs of clothing in department-store windows, at Christmas time if possible – the moving three-dimensional sculptural effects will be amazing, not to mention the glitz, decoration and fashion accessories to be seen.*
▶ *Find some reference material that shows the shapes of fashionable shoes. Draw these shapes, then apply a contemporary design onto them.*
▶ *Research designs from Japanese kimonos and bags. Photocopy or print out interesting designs for your reference. Think about how these designs could be adapted to include surface-designed and painted fabrics as well as image transfer.*

Fashion has been just briefly touched upon in this section. The wealth of cultural and historic fashion traditions, sewing styles and materials could be a rich area of research.

Above and right: **Don't Tell Your Mother** (Val Jackson, UK); **Can He Waltz?** (Val Jackson, UK). Intriguingly shaped fashion textiles mixed with images and words to create memories in stitch. Far right: Fun with modern fashion-model sketches superimposed on an antique log-cabin quilt.

Top left and right (detail): **Modern Woman III** (Jill Flower, UK). Recycled papers and magazines about women, with added buttons, baubles and beads. Above left: Stylized kimono shapes combined with art cloth and photo images. Could this become a wall-hung stitched textile? (Sandra Meech, UK). Left: **Gaga: Demystifying the Celebrity** (Toni Bellamy, UK). Mixed-paper collage and drawings, digitally printed onto cloth.

Fine art

The world of art has been a strong influence on composition in all textile disciplines. Stylized objects in early embroidery, tapestry and the decorative arts were directly influenced by how details in nature, the landscape and everyday life were depicted in early paintings. Art influences how we see and understand design in our environment – consider how early family portraits could have spread the influence and knowledge of new fashions from one country to another. Certainly, our understanding of abstraction in today's stitched textiles is directly related to the world of contemporary art.

From the world of art we learn about:

• **Form and content** The form your textile art takes will take will depend on how your application of the principles of design come together with your choice of materials and stitch techniques to become a resolved piece. The content, on the other hand, is what has inspired the piece in the first place, the research and ideas on a theme – the work that goes on before you start making. Content also refers to the mood, emotion or expressive feeling that you want to convey in your piece of work, whether the subject is realistic or conceptual. Painters have used the idea of form and content in the critique of their work for years, and it could be something to consider in your own textile work as well.

For example, taking the lily flower as an inspiration for textile design, the smooth white and cream/yellow colours and flowing shapes could present many design possibilities. With an interesting composition, an enlarged lily shape could be enough to catch a viewer's initial interest. But imagine how much more interesting it would be if, on closer inspection, there was a hint of words or religious symbolism, perhaps – more detail that would keep the viewer transfixed. On a deeper level, the stitch design itself could send another subtle message – personally, I love the shape of the flower but do not like the smell, so the stitch design might be made up of sharp, jagged lines combined with the smooth shape and subtle colour of the flower and the words. Think in terms of different levels of information in your approach to a subject.

• **Art and symbolism** Pictures and symbols have been illustrated on cloth and used in art as well as in general and mainstream culture for centuries, to reflect wealth and status, convey public information, and for the purposes of ritual. Many of these symbols are universal – the cross, the spiral, the hand or heart shape, for instance. Cultural influences have created a huge set of symbols that we all immediately recognize – the red cross, the stop sign, the signs to symbolize ladies' and gents' toilets, the red, amber and green of traffic lights, for example.

▶ *Create your own symbol from a mark made that is sympathetic to your theme.*

Above, from top: Colourful art on cloth (Kris Michael, Canada); peeling paint on wood (photo Sandra Meech, UK); A child's painting (Warren, age 3). Above: Classic paintings like **The Third of May** by Goya shows movement across the canvas. The arrows indicate how the 'eye' is led in and through the painting.

Left: **Still Life with Orange** (Susan Kirkman, UK, private collection). The use of complementary colours and paint marks in this bold painting engages the viewer immediately. Studying art will always trigger ideas for surface design and stitch.

Above: **Letter Landscape** (Jette Clover, Belgium). Powerful block images
of posters and graffiti with a dynamic use of colour across the quilt.

Graphic design

Book and magazine design, poster art, typography, billboards and logos in advertising saturate our lives, sometimes so much so that we don't notice them. The subtlety of advertising is such that we register the right message without realising. Without getting into the ethics of advertising, we can learn so much about design and composition from it. Every product that is advertised is meant to get the viewer's attention, and we can use some of these methods in stitched-textile composition and presentation. For instance, advertising uses colour with care and research – orange is a 'foody' colour, green refers to growth and money, red evokes passion and love. This type of approach can be adopted by stitched-textile designers to great effect.

Typography and lettering – the curve and shape of individual letters in various fonts – can be an inspiration too. The use of words and lettering in textiles engages viewers as they try to read them. Peeling layers of old posters display a myriad of layered meanings which could be an intriguing subject for layered fabrics with sheers, perhaps.

▶ *Find a double-page layout that you like in a magazine. This should be something modern, with clean lines and white space. Find a way to adapt it and make it your own, with images and copy you have generated. Then consider how you could translate it into a future textile piece.*

▶ *Consider creating a small collage in black and white with words and images on a theme. Add colour with pencil, oil pastel or stitch into the paper (see illustration right).*

Ceramics, glass and mixed media

These disciplines straddle craft and fine art, and some makers in craft disciplines would like recognition in the world of fine art. Although there are those that do not recognize crafts and mixed-media work as art forms, people's perception of art and craft is changing, and we can only hope that, when handcrafted work (stitched, silk-screened and monoprinted, for instance) is well designed, the public will consider it as high a form of art as a painting. Book construction could be classified in this area, too, as many paper sculptures are works of art.

Above, from top: **Avril**, 1893 (Toulouse-Lautrec) and **Salome**, 1894 (Aubrey Beardsley) are instantly recognizable posters. Graphic design plays an influential role in Western life: a torn poster with intriguing mixed messages; a black-and-white collage of images and lettering with a little colour could inspire a stitched textile (Sandra Meech, UK). Left: An example of the use of balance in book design.

Design Class 2
WINDOWS AND WALLS

Windows, grids and facades

- Using a high-contrast black-and-white photograph of a building's façade with a grid of windows as a design source, draw or trace sections in heavy black pen. See illustrations left and below. Make a black-and-white copy and randomly cut through some of the window openings. Lay the copy onto a colour copy of any image of your choice – it does not have to be architectural. See illustrations below.

- Interesting sections you had not noticed before will emerge. These could be photographically transferred onto cloth, or sections applied and the line applied with stitch. This is just a beginning of an interesting design idea. The same effect could be achieved with Photoshop Elements – the drawing becomes a cut-out layer and is then overlaid onto another image. Look at the work of the artist Friedensreich Hundertwasser and see how he used colour and shape in a similar but modern architectural way.

Above: A line drawing from a black-and-white photograph of the Blue Fin building in London and a colourful market scene in the Dordogne are combined. Could this become an art quilt?

 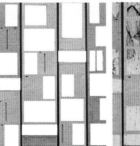 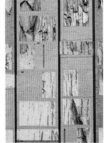

Distressed, textured walls

Another possibility with a modern building facade is to consider the squares and rectangles filled with wall textures – the contrast of rough and smooth. Faded posters on walls, peeling paint or distressed stonework are all favourite subjects for textile artists. Explore different ways of using these textures. Illustrated left are two examples of how buildings and posters can be combined. Firstly, the classic shapes of Tate Modern are simplified and combined with a poster image. This simple composition could easily be translated into fabric and stitch. The second example uses images of a distressed wall and a modern building, simplified and combined using Photoshop. Both effects can also be created with colour photocopies cut out and pasted together.

Right: **Freedom Walls** (Sandra Meech, UK), a woven grid of mixed fabrics that represents the fall of the Berlin Wall.

DESIGN ELEMENTS

The elements of design are the visual tools used to compose a piece of work – line, shape, space, value, colour and texture. The principles of design tell you how to combine these elements skilfully by establishing what works and what does not. They show you the way forward and, with practice, the process becomes intuitive. However, just as important as these tools and principles is that 'gut feeling' – knowing when something just looks 'right'. Children who know nothing about the principles of design can make wonderful, energetic pieces of work naturally, with no inhibitions, by relying on their instincts to guide them.

Once you gain the confidence to use the tools and principles of design naturally, your fears and inhibitions about design will recede, and this will be reflected in your textile work. But bear in mind that design principles are not an absolute science and can be challenged by the maker who has a strong vision of what he wants to achieve. Learning about the elements and principles of design will give you the confidence to make strong compositions and, as you develop your instincts, you'll also get a sense of when you need to bend the 'rules'.

Left: **Rock Fall 2** (Anne Froggatt, UK). Inspired by the colours and details in the landscape of Cumbria, the contrasting circular and linear rock shapes have been created in felt and stitch. Right: **Gesture I** (Lottie Reay, UK). This expressive collage with stitch shows great movement but uses the classic triangular still-life composition.

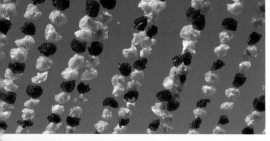

LINE

From the first marks made on cave walls to lines carved in the landscape of prehistoric Peru, man has sought to depict line in his environment in a variety of ways. Line is one of the fundamental elements in stitched textiles.

Line can be curved, straight, diagonal, horizontal, vertical, thick, thin, broken, single or clustered. Lines can become directional tools to guide the viewer into and around the surface of a piece of work. In stitched textiles, line can become stitch, playing a very important role in the flow of the design across the surface.

Straight lines feel static, curved lines flow, and diagonal lines add energy. The contrast between vertical and horizontal lines can create tension. Line can be visible, implied (by a broken or dotted line, for instance), or totally non-existent or imaginary (as a viewer, you are directed by the composition to create a line in your mind, but no line is actually there).

Line can be achieved with any medium: pencil, pen, charcoal, oil pastels, paint and brush or stick, thick and thin nib pens, bleach, knife scrape marks, and so on.

▶ *Look at the lines, straight and curved, in the world around you – in trees, the sides of a guitar, the curves of the human body on or an animal. In architecture or the urban landscape, study the lines found in the textures, curves and angles of historic decoration. Look at lines in household objects. Document these lines in your sketchbook.*

▶ *Create marks related to a personal theme. Draw a single line, then a large one, then small, then draw overlapped and intense lines. Using tracing paper or acetate, overlap lines, then view them through a 'window' to isolate interesting variations in your line clusters – a small area may have strong simplicity, while the whole area may be less interesting or too cluttered.*

▶ *Consider how line can be used to express movement and rhythm across the surface of a piece of work. Look at how Van Gogh used line and marks to show movement in his cypress paintings. Use oil pastels to make rhythmic and expressive lines across your paper.*

▶ *Take a line for a walk. Do this freehand, or sketch on your computer with your mouse. Try doing this exercise to music, making marks in response to what you are hearing. Now do the same exercise with machine stitch.*

▶ *Consider line as a dot. Everything starts with a dot, so start with a dot and allow it to become larger and see what happens. If you are working in stitch, the dot can become a small darning stitch or French knot.*

Hint Don't worry about scale at this point. Many of these exercises could be included in your sketchbook. Try windowing areas for interest: a small area could have the strong simplicity you are searching for, whereas the whole area may be less interesting or too cluttered.

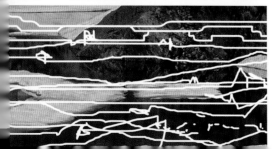

Left, from top: Stripes are everywhere – at festivals, in woods, the skin of a mackerel, stacked tiles and lavender fields, for example. Line that is curved and repeated becomes pattern, seen here with the marks on the fish and ceramic roof tiles. Bottom: Line marks are imposed on an image of melting ice, representing a timeline.

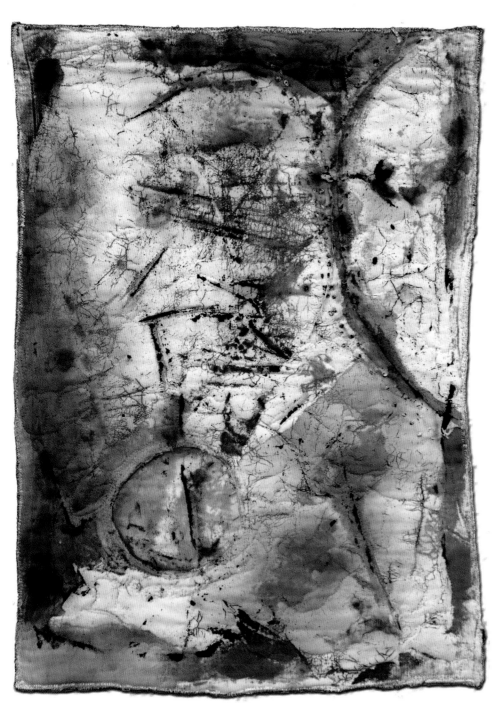

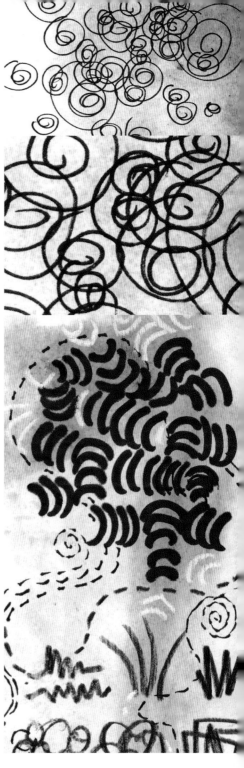

Above: **Sacred Circles** (Maggie Vanderweit, Canada). The 'marks' resemble ancient man-made symbols and reflect a fusion of materials, with painted cloth and stitch. Top right: Line, marks and patterns on a painted background suggest possibilities with stitch. Create a number of different symbols for each theme that is explored. Right: Sketchbook pages are the best place to practise line and pattern. Use painted black-and-white copies for reference.

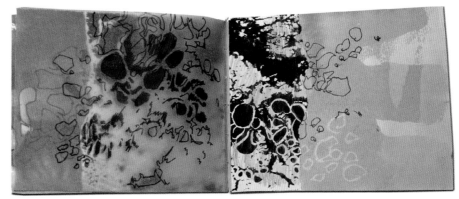

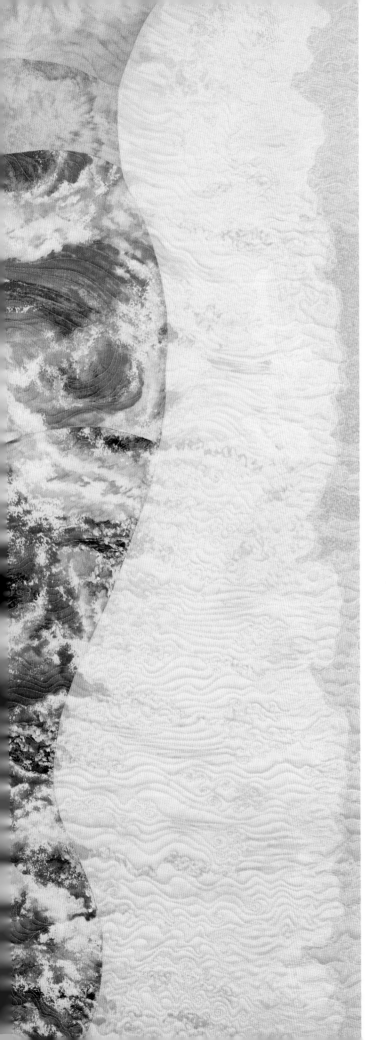

Line as pattern

In sketchbooks, line is used to create tone with cross-hatching, parallel lines or grids, or to divide areas. In nature, the tessellated pavements of Tasmania are a good example of how repeated grids can form a pattern in nature.

▶ *Draw a line and use a photocopier to print it multiple times, reducing and enlarging it for thicker and thinner versions. Print it out on tracing paper and overlay your marks, using the same line repeatedly to form a pattern. Lines traced from the photograph above have been overlaid and cropped to form an interesting pattern. Could this become a design for stitch?*

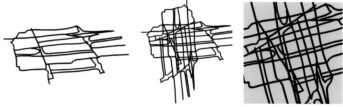

▶ *Find patterns formed with line in the world around you (ploughed furrows, railway tracks, fences or cages, for example). Record these examples in your sketchbook.*

▶ *Study how line as pattern is used in world textiles – African Kuba cloth, for example. Record your findings in your sketchbook.*
▶ *Choose a selection of photographs. Lighten and increase the contrast of black-and-white versions to reveal patterns made with line.*

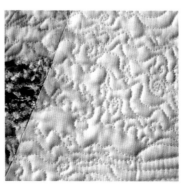

Left: **Breakers (detail)** (Sheena Norquay, UK). Creative line with machine quilting creates added depth in this piece. Detail shown above. The full piece can be seen on page 36.

Left: **Klimt's Garden** (Dwayne Wanner, Canada). Directional lines and rectangular shapes across and through the whole surface keep the viewer engaged. Below: **Marching to a Different Drummer** (Kate Cox, USA). Flowing lines and sharp angles create movement, with the repeat bars suggesting a musical 'beat'. Below left: A collage created using shapes and bars placed at angles.

Directional line in composition

The implied line in fine art is used to suggest where the viewer's eye is to be directed, and can be used in the same way in stitched textile design. In paintings by the Great Masters, implied line is evident – the direction of a sword, a beam of light from above, or the way people are grouped can direct our focus. In this way, a composition becomes a series of invisible directional lines.

▶ *Create a small collage from painted papers in squares, lines and rectangles placed at angles.*

63

SHAPE

When line joins itself, it becomes shape. Shapes can be small, medium and large for variety – if they are the same size, a composition becomes static. They come in many forms – rectangles, circles and stripes, for instance – and can be made up of the positive and negative spaces in a composition.

Shape, when repeated, can become pattern. When shape becomes dimensional, it becomes form – the square becomes a cube, the circle a sphere, and so on.

Shapes are everywhere around us – think of rock strata, leaves and stones and man-made objects such as tools, household items, or (in the landscape) electricity pylons, wind turbines and windows in a high-rise office block (which consist of geometric and repetitive shapes). Shape can be recognisable, distorted, exaggerated or idealistic, abstract, non-objective (a shape that is a suggestion of something else) or express emotion.

Top: **Petra Impressions** (Anne Froggatt, UK). This piece strongly evokes the colour and structures in rock of this ancient city landscape. Detail shown above.

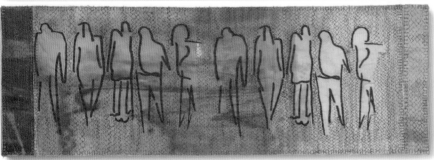

Above: **Morston Silence** (Debbie Lyddon, UK) The circular and linear shapes contrast with the horizontal landscape composition with a strong-but-subtle use of complementary colours. Left: **Café Culture 1 and 2** (Susan Chapman, UK). Dynamic colour immediately attracts attention, and the repeat figure shapes seem to move back and forth on the surface. Below: a Pueblo jar is not only a beautiful shape but is full of line and detailed imagery.

▶ *From magazine examples find some basic shapes – exaggerated or abstract. You may have photos of your own that you can use for this exercise. Scan any interesting shapes you find and create a series of repeat shapes on your computer, then cut and paste the shapes in different sizes to create interesting possibilities for a future composition. On page 70, multiple shapes are influenced by the space around them.*

65

Stripes

Stripes are thicker lines that have become shapes. From decorative textiles to decoration on ancient pots, stripes have been instrumental in creating colour combinations that create movement or depth across the surface. Densely placed stripes can give the illusion of distance, while open stripes seem to advance. Regularly spaced stripes become static, and this fact can be employed to express a theme about confinement, for example.

▶ *Working in a neutral palette of creams or neutral colours, create a series of torn strips of paper. Assemble these together in a collage, then superimpose a dark line drawing on top. How do you feel this should be positioned? How do the lines and stripes work together?*

▶ *Irregular stripes could be a border treatment. Make the strips different widths and the borders asymmetrical. Border exercises with strips and stripes are on pages 118–120.*

Top: **Domestic Mapping: Crow 3** (Cas Holmes and Anne Kelly, UK) explores the subtlety of recycled materials. Above: A line imprint of a Pueblo jar over a collage of neutral-coloured papers.

Squares and rectangles

Squares and rectangles have given an order to life and art through the ages, and are among the first shapes we remember (as windows, buildings, tile floors, books and so on). In textiles the 30cm (12in) block square is fundamental to quilt design (see the design class on rotated squares for block design on page 80.)

It can be challenging to group squares and rectangles together without the composition looking busy, unplanned or cluttered. Working with a grid of squares and rectangles could help to bring some order and structure to such a composition.

▶ *Photograph squares and rectangles found in nature or the urban landscape. Select a photograph that inspires an idea that could be developed further as a textile piece.*
▶ *Weave and glue together strips of paper torn from painted pages, colour photocopies (a good combination might be two painted papers and one full-page colour photocopy) and, perhaps, magazine pages. Consider how your results could inspire a series of work.*
▶ *Repeat a pattern of squares (made from either paper or fabric) on a dark or light background, adding lines that could later inform stitch. Scan and transfer the pattern onto fabric (or print it onto the fabric), then add stitch. Work that is too symmetrical can become too comfortable, so it might be good to isolate an angled section or bring a touch of dynamic colour into the equation.*

Above left: **Considering Red** (Jette Clover, Belgium). Each piece is a media 'story' with a dynamic hint of red. Above, from top: Squares and rectangles are everywhere around us; torn and woven magazine papers give a variety of interesting design options; a composition with writing and images on fabric with stitch.

Curves and circles

Circles and curves are everywhere in the world around us. They can be organic and asymmetrical, or arranged in a repeat pattern. Circles can be calming and peaceful, or dynamic and powerful. There is something comforting about circular shapes and the eye is drawn to them. Curves, whether real or suggested, will always strengthen a composition as they encourage the viewer's eye to move around the surface. From the natural curve of the human body, markings on tropical fish or distant hills on the horizon to man-made designs – musical instruments, architecture and furniture – the curve is always present and provides an uplifting foil to the regimentation of straight lines.

-Left: **Evolution 1** (Maggie Barber, UK) There is so much to captivate the viewer in this piece. The circle shapes are repeated with the use of French knot embroidery marks, contrasting with the angled stitch marks across the whole surface. The vertical line also divides the composition, yet links the shapes. Detail shown below.

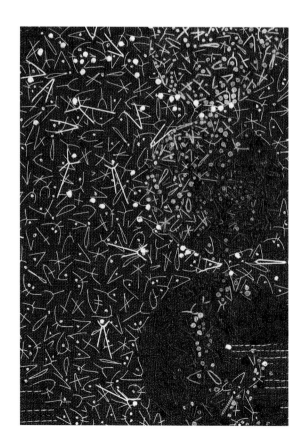

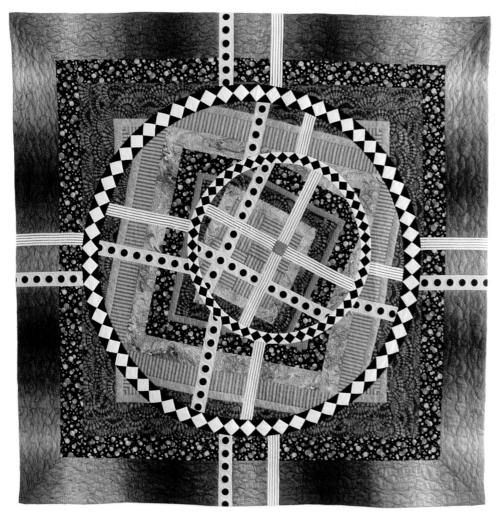

Left: **Treasure Vault** (John Willard, Canada). What initially appears to be a symmetrical composition is not. The cross/circle shapes are rotated slightly, adding movement and interest. Below: Candy stripes and spirals (photo Sandra Meech, UK). Bottom: Paper collage made with strips.

▶ Create a collage using strips of painted paper (or fabric) cut into different widths. Trace the strip composition onto paper and practise cutting curves first this way. Then cut the collage horizontally into three to five curved sections (as illustrated right) in soft curves in different widths and reassemble them into a new collage, mixing the order of the cut sections – some could be upside down. Use the rule of thirds (see page 35) when placing your horizontal strips. One strip alone could be effective as a design.

▶ Dots are circles. Small dot patterns can act as a tone – different-sized dots can create their own dynamics, very large dots become circles and can be real or suggested. Try a few illustrations of this on your own to show the difference.

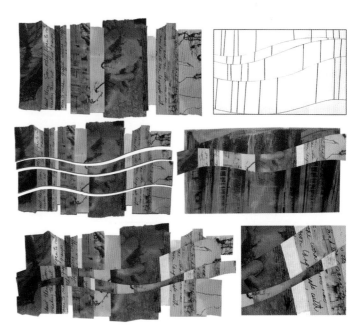

SPACE

The shapes you create in a piece of work are positive spaces, and the areas between and around them are the negative spaces. Attention to both is important in good composition. Creating the illusion of space and depth is a challenge in flat stitched-textile disciplines, so we have to achieve this in other ways. In landscape composition, depth can be achieved by full detail in the foreground and directional movement in the mid-ground that directs the eye further back to important information on the horizon. You can see great emphasis placed on the use of space to create depth in posters and modern page design.

Size (scale) and proportion

The scale of compositional elements is important. They can be big or small, and their size is determined by their relationship to other compositional elements, or by how they fill the frame. The proportion of these elements of composition – if they are larger or smaller than the expected 'norm' – can communicate something specific and dramatic.

▶ *Play with the size and proximity of a shape, vary its size and see how different the compositions can be. Use any surface materials for interest. Consider developing one idea into a small stitched piece.*

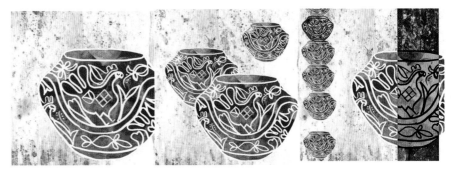

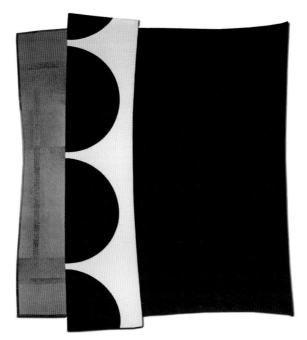

Above: **Symbols** (Amarjeet Nandhra, UK). Though the circles are repeated, they are all different, and seem to move in and out of the greyed surface. Blue and gold thread has been added to one of them. Right: **Apocalypso** (Katriina Flensburg, Sweden). This dramatic art quilt uses both circular and rectangular shapes to their best advantage. The red strip at the edge provides a good contrast to the stark black and cream of the rest of the piece. Above right: Examples testing out various compositions for a picture of a Pueblo jar, created in Photoshop.

Above: Examples testing out various compositions for a picture of a Navajo jug, created in Photoshop. Opposite, top: **Come Join Us** (Mirjam Pet-Jacobs, Netherlands), This piece's strong composition is a wonderful example of positive and negative as the stylized people move back and forth.

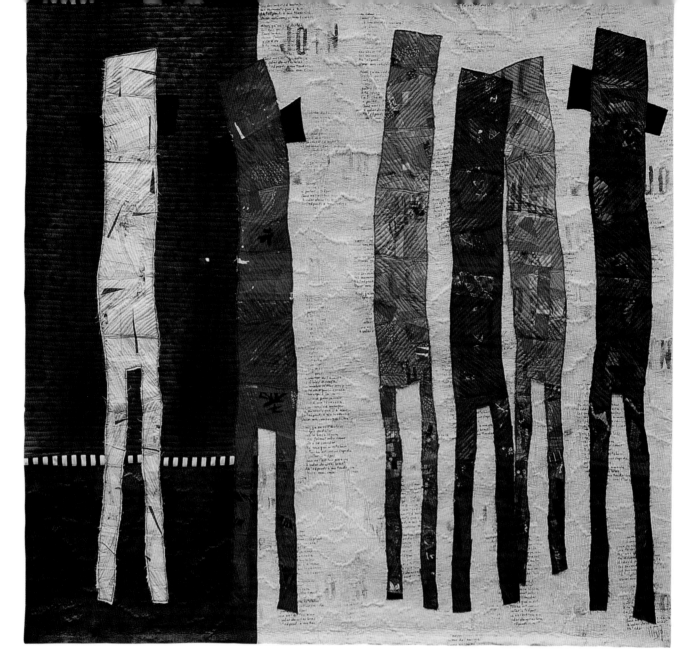

Ideas to consider

• **Notan** is a Japanese design concept that involves the juxtaposition of light and dark shapes. Using cut-paper shapes in black and white is the easiest way to create this effect, or you could try working with black-and-white shapes on your computer. An isolated area of the finished piece could spark compositional ideas (see the illustration right).

• **Positive and negative space** Thinking about positive and negative shapes in relation to your personal theme could suggest a dynamic composition. Also, fine artists often look at a planned composition in terms of positive and negative spaces. This can be done with collage to assess how well a composition works.

• **Create contrasts with density and space** Some elements, clumped together, will be dynamic, but only if there is space around them.

• **Contrast with light and dark** This can be very dramatic – think how emotional black-and-white photography can be.

Above: Here, the same Pueblo jar is split into a positive/negative design, with a separate detail selected. Could this become a design using complementary colours in dyed fabric?

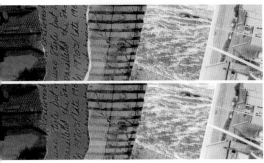

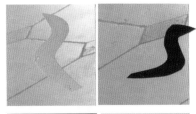

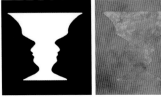

VALUE

The tonal values and contrasts in your work are critical when it comes to making a composition work. The lights and darks contribute more to the success of the overall surface design than colour, shape or texture. It is the contrast of tones that will really capture the viewer's interest and helps to provide the path around the surface of the piece. Using tonal values can be the best way of creating a strong focal point. Never make sections that have a similar tonal value the same size as this will make the composition weak, confusing and perhaps even boring. Colour, texture and embellishment are important, but it is essential to think about the dynamics of a composition first in terms of tonal values. Plan where the lights and darks will be in your composition from the start. This can be done with sketches or mini collages.

Tonal values can be used in many ways. They can create a mood – for example, very light values can create an uplifting feeling, while dark tones can be dark and depressing. Contrasting dark and light shapes can provide the 'wow' factor of surprise, creating the effect of something extraordinary and unplanned. Strong positive and negative shapes can trick your eye when the positive and negative are in the same proportion, while graduating tonal value can create the illusion of depth. In stitched-textile pieces, graduation could be achieved by using dyed fabrics.

▶ *Tear grey magazine papers and layer them in a collage to create a distant horizon. Find magazine papers in different shades of grey and tear as indicated in the picture shown. Imposing a 50 per cent grey value 'window' frame will show the contrast from dark to light.*
▶ *Gather a collection of your favourite fabrics or paper swatches with different textures and patterns. Photograph them in colour, then convert the resulting pictures to black and white. What do you notice about their appearance now? How do they relate to one another tonally?*
▶ *Take a colour photograph and convert it to black and white on your computer. Do you notice more shapes and tones once colour is removed? Isolate an area to explore – squint for an out-of-focus view of it, which can reveal tonal values and help you determine simple shapes.*
▶ *A photograph of an archway in Beaumont, France (below) is viewed in different ways for tonal value. First the photo is converted to black and white, and distinct shapes begin to appear. (It is always helpful to convert an inspirational photo image into black and white to see detail and shape.) Then a 'posterizing' filter (in Photoshop Elements) is used, which breaks the surface tones into three to five planes. A detail at this stage already feels abstract, and could inspire a future textile.*

Above: Value exercises. From top: Using tone to suggest depth in a landscape; tonal values of photos or fabric seen in black and white; two examples of how values can appear – on the left, they are similar as tones blend together, on the right the contrast is strong; do you see the vase or the faces? Both are easy to see in black and white, but more difficult when rendered in colours with similar tonal values.

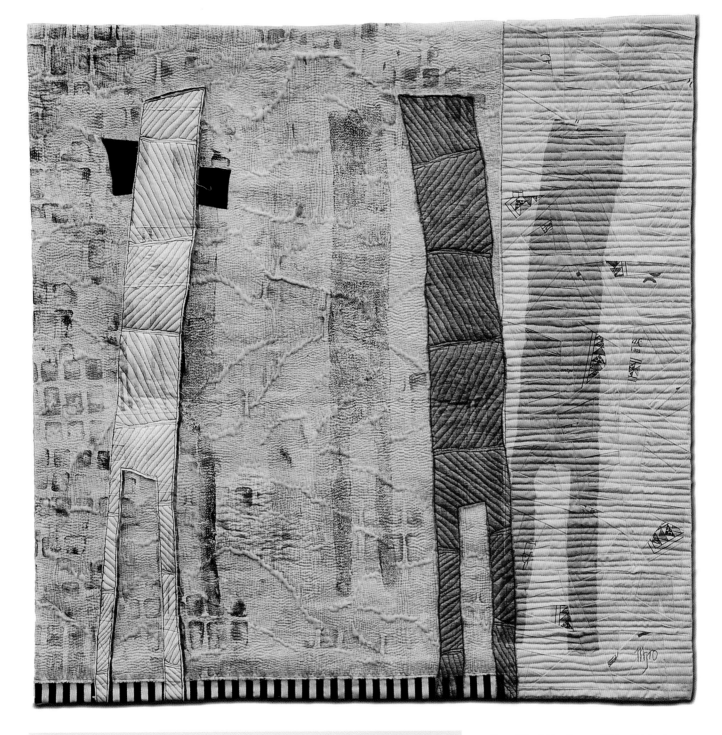

Hint

Odd numbers Any object that we want to draw attention to in our work should be surrounded by an even number of objects. So you could have one main focus and two others shadowing the object, or one main focus and four others shadowing it.

Triangles are aesthetically pleasing, so arranging objects in the shape of a triangle works well in composition (see page 110). Still-life compositions and portraits often contain a triangular element.

Leaving space on the surface gives viewers a chance to breathe and collect their thoughts. Space can also suggest movement. Think of a solitary person walking from left to right on the canvas – the white space indicates movement.

Simplify Less is more. Keeping to a main focus will always be dynamic. Keep the surface uncluttered.

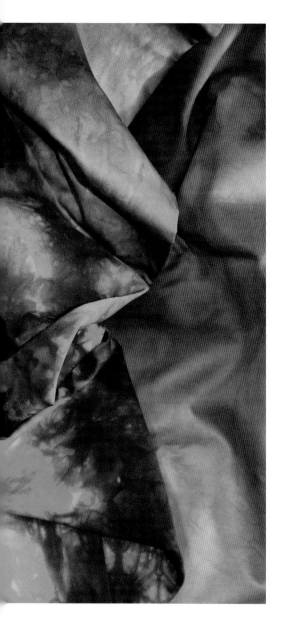

COLOUR

No review of the elements of design would be complete without addressing colour. Every day we see thousands of colours – colours that give inspiration, awaken our imagination and stimulate emotion. How you use colour makes your work individual. Studying the colour wheel and bearing in mind simple rules will help you to organize groups of colours, show their relationship to each other and transmit emotions to the viewer. The absence of colour or working in neutrals can also be dynamic and expressive. Dramatic monochromatic, black and white or neutral textile works with just a little accent colour can be the strongest pieces in an exhibition.

► *Work with a single colour photograph on your computer for this exercise. Make multiple copies, then try creating different colour effects in each copy. You can reduce the intensity of hue, lighten, darken, make a copy in black and white, make a monochrome copy in colour, oversaturate one copy or create a high-contrast black-and-white copy. Experiment. In Photoshop Elements it is also possible to invert the colour. Now assess the mood of each copy – how do the copies differ and why? This exercise might inspire colour approaches in future textile pieces (see below).*

The meanings of colours

Humans have, over the centuries and across all cultures, attributed certain characteristics, moods and emotions to colours. These associations are used in design. In poster art and advertising, these universal colour associations are used to attract attention and evoke emotion in order to transmit a message to the viewer. Traditionally, warm and cool colour combinations evoke certain emotions, but to entice the viewer, it can be effective to use very different colour arrangements – consider how the Impressionists sometimes used a complementary palette (the opposite hues on the colour wheel) to disarm the viewer. Look in magazines to see how colour is used to attract attention or evoke a mood.

Yellow: joy, happiness, energy
Gold: wealth, prosperity, success
Orange: food, power, creativity, warmth
Brown: earthy, natural, wholesome, also decay
Red: bravery, passion, heat, energy
Pink: love, tenderness, relaxation
Purple: royalty, magic, mystery, good judgement
Blue: cold, sky, ocean, heaven, peace, truth, conservatism
Turquoise: youth, health, confidence, warm sea, purity
Green: nature, fertility, life, growth, money, healing
Black: the absence of colour, mystery, death, elegance, evil
Grey: sorrow, isolation, narrow-mindedness, conservatism
White: purity, peace, virginal love, wholeness, truth and, in some cultures, death

Top: Colourful hand-dyed cotton (Heidi Stolle-Weber, Germany). Above: the same view with different Photoshop treatments. Top row: the original image; lightened; monochrome in blue; with saturated colour. Bottom row: in sepia tones; darkened; posterized; with inverted colour. Each variation evokes a different mood.

Colour schemes

There have been entire books written on the great variety of colour combinations found in art, interior design, advertising, fashion, and so on, but it is best to keep your colour schemes simple. Experimenting with bright colours, greyed shades or pale tints of colours with swatches of fabric, paint cards or torn magazine papers can be a good place to start.

▶ *If you haven't already, begin a collection of references for colour combinations from magazines and personal photographs. Study this collection frequently to absorb the information you have gathered. Look for warm and cool colours used together, analogous colours, active and passive colours, monochromatic schemes and the use of black and white and neutrals.*

The relationship between colour and tonal value

Consider a value scale of a series of coloured shapes, then the same series shown in black and white. In the black-and-white version, some of the greys will be indistinguishable from one another, yet in colour, the differences can be seen. In the black-and-white scale, yellow, although a bright, eye-popping colour, will be seen as white or 10 per cent grey. Red, another bright colour, will be seen as a very dark grey tone. For this reason, colour offers a much broader visual range of meanings, moods and contrasts than black and white.

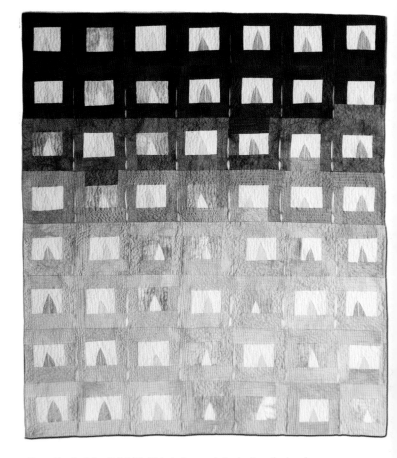

Above: **Track of the Point** (Pia Welsch, Germany). Graduation of colour from bright to dark works well in this piece as the repeat blocks appear to come forward. Below: the traditional colour wheel created in photographs and fabrics.

Above, top: The tonal value of a red flower looks very different when it is viewed in black and white. Above: Analogous collages in magazine paper with a twist – hot colours with a touch of cold, cool colours with hot red, and a group of neutrals distinguished by varied pattern.

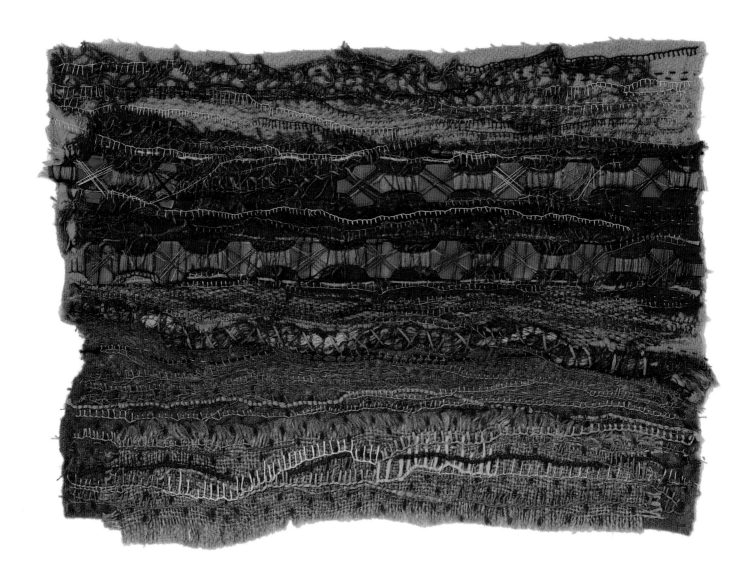

Above: **Landscape, Storm** (Annette Collinge, UK). This piece uses complementary colours.

Colour dominance

Variety in the proportions of colours used (having different amounts of various colours) will make a pleasing and balanced colour scheme that can provoke emotion and be strong and daring, or subtle and evocative.

▶ *In this exercise, you will isolate colour choices from a photograph. Using a window template and choosing small areas, isolate areas showing at least six to eight different colours. Now study those combinations. The combination could be subtle or bright. Analogous colour combinations work well. Consider the use of shades, tints or neutral colours (greys, creams) also. Look at the proportions of colours in the photo area and find the same proportion in coloured magazine papers (as illustrated). This is a useful exercise in simplifying reference information and seeing how colours work with each other. It could be repeated again on another section of the same photograph for a different combination to create a different mood.*

Far left: Nine different colours appear in this cropped photograph (Sandra Meech, UK). Left: The same nine colours shown in pages torn from magazines.

Colour relationships

• **Simultaneous contrasts** When solid-coloured or greyed areas of different values are adjacent to one another, the differences between them become evident (a). The illustration right shows how the areas look darker or lighter depending on their values. Thin bars at the edge have lessened the contrast between them (b). In textiles, this technique can be applied by piecing or adding rows of stitch to blend the division of colour.

• **Contrasting values** A colour will look darker on a light background and lighter on a dark one. If you use two swatches of the same colour and place one on a light background and the other on a dark one, it will be hard to believe they are exactly the same colour (c).

• **Contrasts in grey** Grey is especially influenced by the colour next to it – it will take on the colour nearby, as you can see below (d).

a
b
c

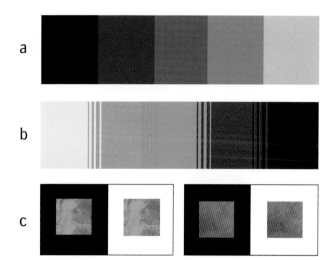

d

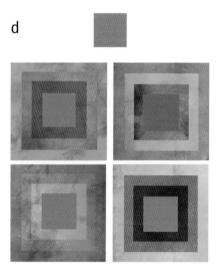

Above: The contrast of colours used next to each other can also create added dimension as shapes vibrate back and forth. Right: **Cathedral Town, Harvest Time** (Alicia Merrett, UK). Vibrant colour and the shapes of this stylized aerial view of a West Country cathedral town are captivating. The roads and lines between the fields also help to create directional movement.

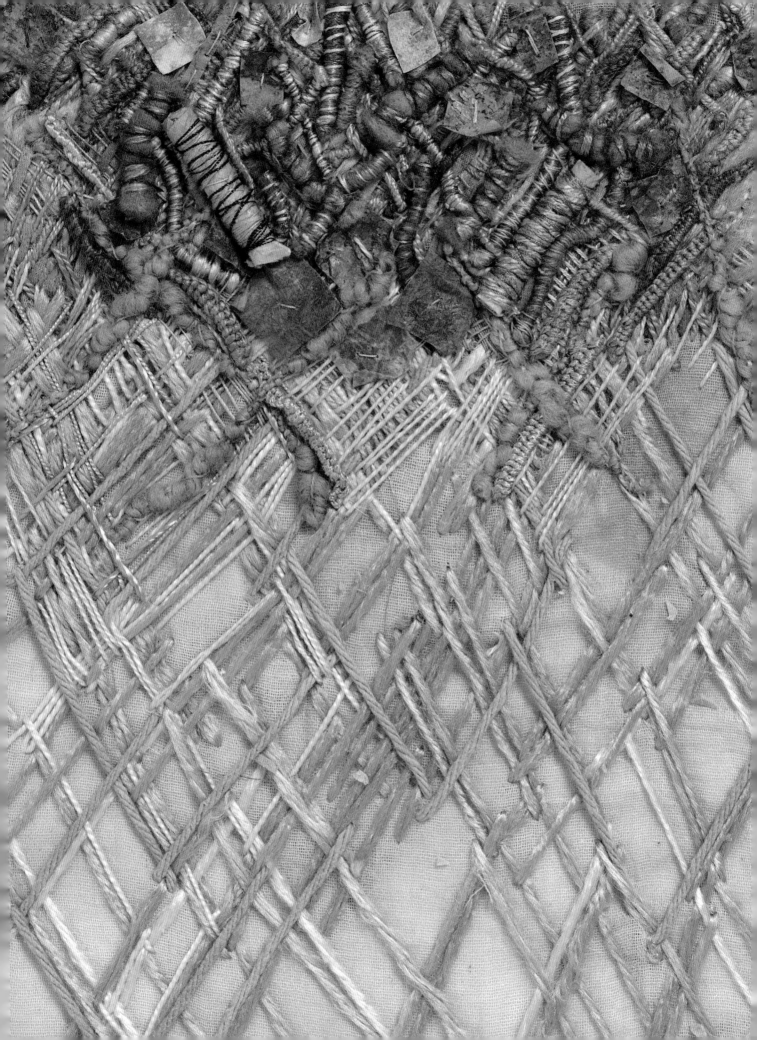

TEXTURE AND PATTERN

Considering this book is intended for lovers of stitch and fabric, texture might have been the first element of design in this section. When a piece of fabric has been pieced, layered, applied or cut with added stitch, the surface becomes a texture. It is, however, important to consider how the surface will be designed at the same time. Good composition is essential, even when the work is highly textured, embellished or dimensional.

There are two types of texture. One is tactile and real, due to how the cloth and surface feels, the embellishment that is added or how dimensional it might look after stitching. The other style of texture is visual – there is no actual texture on the surface, but the illusion of it is created by a pattern or the use of repeat colour on the surface.

Quilters enjoy cotton prints, both traditional and contemporary in nature, or learn different dye, stamp, and print effects to create their own fabrics. Contemporary embroiderers might practise surface techniques that include dense stitch or dimensional layered materials (papers, plastics, metals, wool or fibres with raw edges). Weavers, on the other hand, are doing both – creating a pattern that is both tactile and visual with built-up wool and thread textures. Another style of fabric could be the painted or printed cloth – ranging from Abstract Expressionist painterly styles to painted repeat patterns (think about gutta resists and silk painting, for example). Visual pattern and collage on cloth is also seen more and more with the use of digital imagery in the commercial textile industry.

▶ *Look at some of the reference material you have collected so far – an ethnic pattern with a contemporary twist might be interesting, or photographs of textures or painted and dyed cloth. Isolate a 2.5cm (1in) square of detail. Using photocopies of your detail, first repeat the detail to create a pattern, then rotate the pattern 15 times (as shown below) to see another pattern emerge. (Using your computer can make this exercise quicker.)*
▶ *Select a traditional quilt block and make it more contemporary using any line or imagery you have developed so far in your exercises. The log-cabin sample shown below uses pale black-and-white and colour photos as a starting point.*

Left: **Harvest** (Jen Chamberlain, UK). Textures, pattern and colours reminiscent of fields in autumn. Above right: an array of discharge-dyed and printed cloth with a variety of marks. Centre right: Can you find the square from the photo far right that has been rotated and repeated? With constant repetition a design pattern emerges. Right: using black-and-white, light and coloured images, a log-cabin block has been created. This could suggest a quilt with a traditional block design using digital imagery – a mixture of old and new.

Design Class 3
CONTEMPORARY ROTATED BLOCK DESIGNS

Traditional quilting blocks are many and varied and there should be something to suit everyone. But you may want to create a new style of block yourself. Here is a simple way to create some interesting repeat effects with simple piecing techniques. Remember that the design at this stage is just made with paper, but imagine what the end result might be like in dyed, painted, stamped or printed fabrics in addition to image transfer on cloth. Work on a small scale first and see if you like the results.

▶ *With one of these suggested block designs as a starting point, you can see what happens when each corner becomes the centre – a completely different block. Once you have created a master block, locate points a, b, c and d at each corner. This will make it easier to rotate the squares to create a new block. When the rotating process is repeated many times, another pattern emerges.*

You will need:
- White copy paper
- Black felt pens and pencils
- Coloured pencils
- Scissors and a knife
- Cutting board and ruler
- Painted paper from black-and-white copies
- Colour copies on a theme (at least four copies of one image to make four blocks)
- Glue stick
- A camera is useful to record different arrangements

Remember, these arrangements can also (with practice) be created in Photoshop.

Above: A colourful Mola textile is the inspiration for this rotated block design (photograph Sandra Meech, UK). Right: Suggested block designs to try for this exercise. Far right: The same block in groups of four, rotated from a different centre. The bottom row is another variation, giving different results. Try this exercise with coloured photocopies and painted papers.

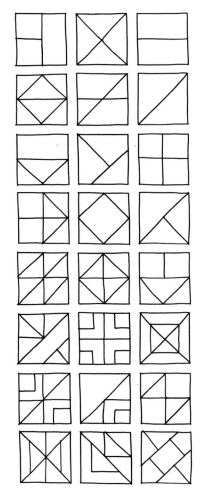

Above: Another created block variation that has been rotated on itself. Remember that if the block is multiplied as well as rotated, a pattern will begin to emerge (see page 79).

Abstract designs

Working with square shapes and abstracts might suggest patchwork and quilting, but these shapes can be adapted to any discipline. Repeat shapes can be seen in embroidery and mixed-media applications as well as tapestry, weaving and feltmaking.

Straight lines

Using a simplified square detail from a photo source, create a new simple square design. Add points a, b, c and d in the four corners and rotate as before, to give a dynamic design.

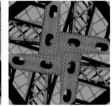
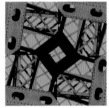
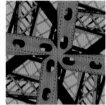

Above and left: Rotated design inspired by a photograph of the Burlington Canal Lift Bridge in Ontario, Canada.

Curved shapes

Curved shapes can also be used within a block inspired by a photo source. The resulting block could also be rotated on itself in the same way, giving endless possibilities.

When taking your work into stitch, a block using straight lines will be easier to create with simple piecing techniques. Curves will offer more of a challenge, but not an impossible one, and worth trying. For all of these design exercises, the composition style would be considered an 'overall' pattern. Sometimes just using the same colour repeatedly will give a unified strength to the end textile piece, or at other times you could vary the colour to create depth and movement back and forth. For more composition styles in textile art see sketchbooks on page 29.

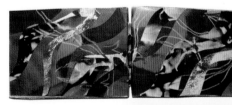

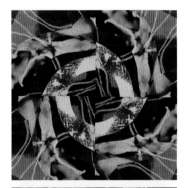

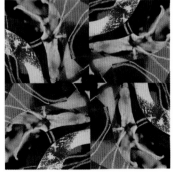

Above and right: A square taken from a sketchbook (based on curves and including pictures of Australian plants with added line in white China marker) was rotated on itself to create a whirlwind design.

DESIGN PRINCIPLES

Just as we have to organize aspects of our lives – by prioritizing what needs to be done, but keeping variety for the sake of interest – our textiles need structure and interest as well. There are tried-and-tested design methods that can be employed to bring both structure and interest to our compositions. Using focal points or a centre of interest and contrast effectively, evoking movement and rhythm in your work, and creating harmony and balance, will help you to develop dynamic, exciting and strong compositions.

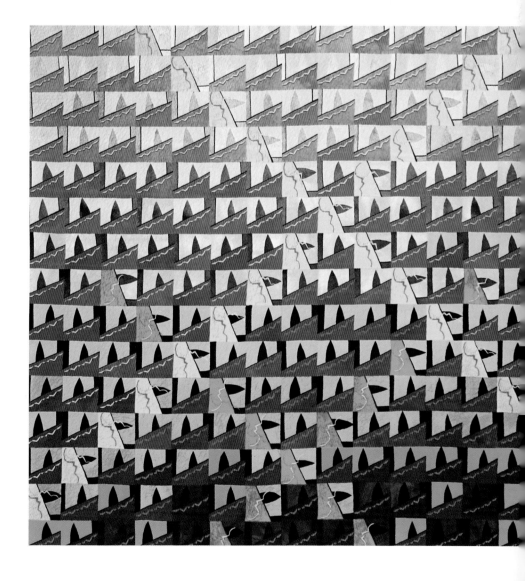

Left: **Fishy Photo** (Sandra Meech, UK) Colour manipulated in Photoshop Elements. Perhaps the placement of the Fibonacci spiral could suggest a cropped area. Right : **Oval #48 × 2** (Pia Welsch, Germany). A strong use of colour contrasts and geometric design makes this composition dynamic.

DOMINANCE

Finding a centre of interest or emphasis is one of the most important aspects of good design. The best way to engage a viewer to stop and look at your work in depth is to have a point of emphasis. That focal point can be overt or suggested; it could be a shape or a spark of colour positioned in a strategic place. If there are too many focal points, or the surface is too busy, there will be no point for the eye to settle on. Remember the rule of thirds (see page 35) and keep it in mind when you are looking at textile art, or indeed any images, in the future.

▶ *Use the rule of thirds to achieve a centre of interest. After establishing the position of the main focal point, place a smaller focal point in the opposite intersection to that of the dominant focal point. Consider this rule and take it to extremes. If there is something of interest on all four of the intersections of the horizontal and vertical lines of the rule of thirds, the focus is back to the centre, creating a 'bull's eye' design. This can also be dynamic if there are little areas of interest across the surface to keep the viewer looking. Using painted papers, colour and black-and-white photocopies, try some compositions yourself. Many could be the inspiration for a larger textile piece in the future.*
▶ *Look at some eye-catching posters or a magazine spread to find the centre of interest. Consider how the placement of a logo, headline or main photograph is often situated in a dynamic position on a page – does this rely on the rule of thirds? If not, why do you think the position is dynamic?*

Emphasis by isolation

Separating one element or shape from the other parts in the composition will emphasize it. By varying the intensity of the shape, its value or colour in a composition, this technique can create dynamic textile design.

▶ *Look for examples of analogous colours in magazine page layouts or works of art and study the placement of colours – do you think the compositions work? If so, why? Notice how a composition comprised of cool or warm colours with a touch of the opposite colour will always be strong.*

Top left: The rule of thirds imposed on an image of West Bay, Dorset. Many viewfinders on digital cameras will provide help with good composition. The horizon and lines of perspective lead directly to the pink building and harbour. Left, second and third down: The images of grapes on the vine and the steps down to the beach both focus on a dominant area in the photo. Far left and left: A photo of an alleyway in France is cropped with L-shaped viewfinders so more detail is seen. Remember how important directional lines are in the composition of a stitched textile.

Placement for emphasis

Using photography, we can easily see how effectively the placement of
shapes can affect a composition. Consider the difference between a
central position for a focal point and one that is asymmetrical.
Sometimes, a single element (shape or line) can be dramatic with
space around it. Bear in mind that a focal point can be very obvious
or very subtle. The more experience you gain in placing important
elements in a composition, the easier you will find it to make your
textile pieces simple yet dynamic.

▶ *Working with your own photographs on the computer or with
L-shaped viewfinders (see opposite page), explore how an image
can be cropped to increase the emphasis of a shape or focal point.*
▶ *Create a collage in paper, fabric or both in which the emphasis is
obvious but much more subtle than in the previous exercise. This can
be achieved if the elements are kept simple and dramatic. Remember
– less is more.*

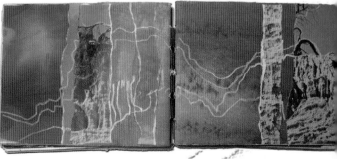

Right: **Cacophony** (Dwayne Wanner, Canada) The coloured shapes and the use of the vertical lines create movement and interest throughout this quilt. Below: A monoprint with repeat pattern and shape has no real focal point, but creates interest with circles and lines across the surface (Kris Michael, Canada). Middle: An impasto acrylic painting with dots of colour for movement (see exercise below). Bottom: Photo and painted-paper 'bits' across a sketchbook page.

Absence of a focal point

Sometimes, it is the absence of a dominant centre of interest that creates a dynamic design. In this scenario, more attention may be given to colour or directional movement to keep the viewer's eye flowing across the surface. Light, shade and shadow are important factors in such compositions, too. Digitally printed repeat patterns with no focal point are often displayed in gallery spaces – it is the way they are hung, and the negative space around them, that will factor into the overall design and composition.

Abstract Expressionist painting often does not seem to have a focus, but the artist may cleverly have included a hint of colour or directional movement that leads the eye around the canvas. Jackson Pollock's paintings are exuberant with what appear random marks across a huge canvas, until your eye picks up bright red daubs that take your attention across the canvas. John Constable, the famous British landscape painter, used the same method, giving farmers in distant fields scarlet coats, which became tiny dots of colour that did not detract from the rest of the composition.

▶ *Create an Abstract Expressionist-style painting in thick impasto made using a palette knife with acrylic paint (see above left). Use only one colour for the bulk of the painting, adding tiny daubs of bright colour across the plane. Such a technique can evoke strong emotions without utilizing a strong focal point.*

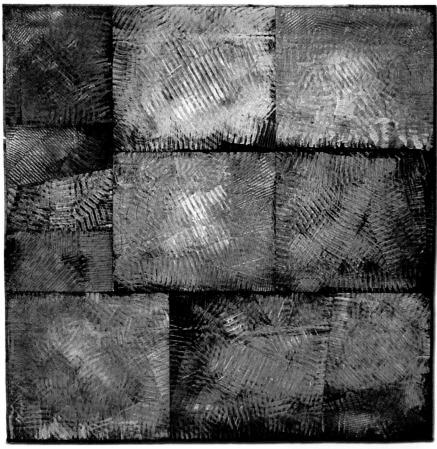

Left: **Raku** (Katriina Flensburg, Sweden) (detail shown below) is very reminiscent of the iridescent colours of raku in ceramics. The glints of orange and purple contrast with the neutral, greyed tones of this art quilt. Below: a colour contrast gives a positive/negative effect in these sketchbook pages. Bottom: A photo taken by chance near Newport, Rhode Island. Size, shape and colour contrast between a sailing boat and the QEII (Sandra Meech, UK).

CONTRAST

Contrast is often shown on its own as a very strong principle of design. We have looked at how contrast can be achieved in relation to a centre of interest, but there are many other ways in which to show dynamic contrast in a composition – for instance, the use of light and dark, warm and cool colours, angled and straight, large and small, rough and smooth. Contrast affects balance, scale, rhythm and unity. A whole theme behind a theme is a conceptual use of contrasts.

Emphasis using contrast

Using contrasting lines, shapes and light and dark areas can make a focal point or centre of interest more dominant. For example, you can have two shapes that are exactly the same size in a composition, but one will dominate more than the other due to its colour or pattern.

In textiles, the contrast of types of fabric can be the making of a piece. Sheers juxtaposed with heavily printed or painted cotton or woven fabrics, smooth silks next to rougher linens, or textured wools placed beside smooth pleated cotton could all look stunning.

Right: **Ebb and Flow** (Kate Cox, USA). Circles, squares and rectangles create movement in this quilt. Above: Harvested wheat in France could provide design inspiration; the lamp for a lighthouse with curves and reflections.

Above: The colour was swapped on these two images of hot, dry Australian soil and melting ice in the Arctic, which could suggest textile work on global warming.

My many visits to Australia over the years continue to inspire me. I am especially intrigued by the landscape – the dry, cracked, red soil, blue skies, grey-green eucalyptus trees. The Australian landscape contrasts in colour to my work based on melting ice, which contains icy blue/turquoise, greys and white. Global warming is affecting all parts of the world. I was struck by how its effects on the Australian dried soil, broken into segments, are very similar to the patterns evident in the ice when it melts. I find it fascinating how these contrasting landscapes have echoes of each other.

Consider some contrasts in subjects that are close to your heart – perhaps something inspired by a trip or experience. Shapes alone (doors, windows, etc) can be a starting point, as can surface textures (such as distressed, peeling walls or brickwork).

Contrasting moods can also be interesting. For instance, a busy piece of art cloth might be difficult to place in a piece of work, but the contrast offered by a calmer piece might allow a section of the busy cloth to provide an interesting focal point. Dyed, painted and screen-printed sections of cloth could work in the same way. (It can be interesting to look at the underside of a busy cloth for a calmer surface pattern.) Sheers will also diffuse and calm busy information to provide contrast.

▶ *Photographs will often reveal details of contrasts that we do not see immediately. Take a look at the lighthouse lamp above left, for example. Look through your collection of photographs to isolate sections of contrasting textures.*

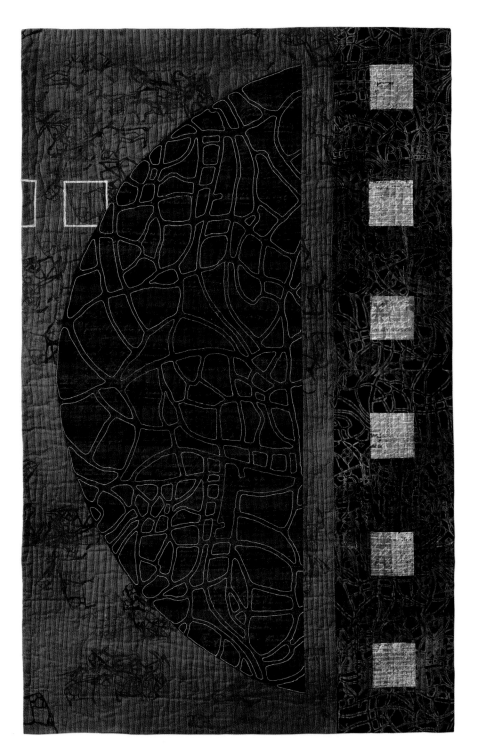

Above left: **Urban Transcript** (Eszter Bornemisza, Hungary). The simple squares and a semi-circular shape contrast with the detail and movement of the stitch lines, which reflect old city maps. Above right, from top: Ceramic tiles in France could provide ideas with contrasting shapes and light and shade; the repetition of shape and colour in stacked roof tiles; grasses and reeds contrast with water and reflections, resembling a strange, illegible script.

HARMONY

Harmony in a composition can be achieved when colours that are adjacent on the colour wheel (analogous) are used together, or if there is a similarity in the value of the colours, lines, shapes or scale of the elements in the composition, which can make the piece pleasing and comfortable. Sometimes, a slight variation of these elements could be included to add interest, such as a different texture, a wobbly line, a brighter colour or a colour that is from the opposite side of the colour wheel (complementary).

BALANCE

Balance is also an important principle to consider in the composition of textile pieces. The effective placement of elements of a similar weight can provide equilibrium. These elements (line, shape, tone, etc) can be symmetrical or similar, opposing or contrasting but, together, these elements create a unified whole. Balance can also be asymmetrical – the elements are unevenly divided but are visually comfortable. 'Balance' can also refer to similar amounts of colour, values (tones), shapes or texture across the surface.

When it comes to achieving balance in a piece of work, getting it right takes practice, but it will become more natural the more you explore the various possibilities.

▶ *Using some commercial quilting cotton, cut a number of squares and arrange them together in a variety of compositions to see how balanced they are next to each other. You will need less of the bright, busy patterns and more of the plainer, textured ones.*

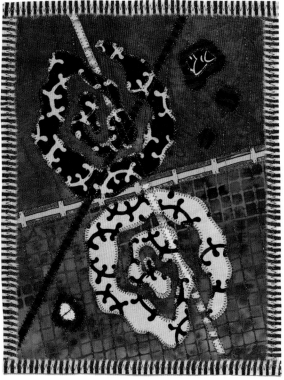

Top left: **Spring Snow** (Cas Holmes, UK). This stitched textile is calm and harmonious, but the heat of the red throughout, representing the warmth of spring, is well placed for interest. Left: **Self Encounter #4** (David Walker, USA). Colour and shapes both contrast with and complement each other in this dynamic small stitched textile. There is more to see on closer inspection (private collection).

Above: **Silent Voice** (Sandra Meech, UK) is inspired by forests that have been loved and lost. Climate change has caused an infestation of pine beetles, killing miles of woodlands in North America. This art quilt represents this loss through the use of positive and negative images.

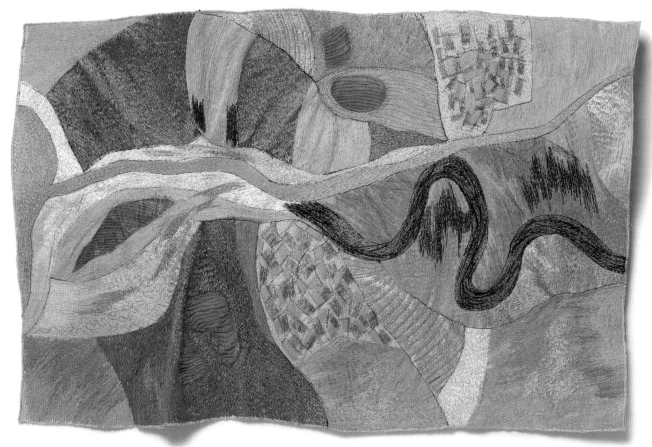

MOVEMENT

Being able to describe movement across the surface in an art quilt is a useful skill, as it allows you to create a dynamic, energetic composition. Movement can be very emotive, disturbing, disarming and unsettling or energizing and exciting, and it could become an important feature in a themed piece of work.

There are three main types of movement in composition – horizontal movement, vertical movement and diagonal movement.

• **Horizontal** The horizon line, whether it resembles a landscape or not, is restful and calming – our eye always seeks out a horizon line if it can. A horizon line also allows you to show layers of information, the most visible being in the foreground, and create the illusion of depth.

• **Vertical** Vertical lines usually suggest buildings, figures or growth, and can be very strong elements in a composition. They can also suggest the end of a movement, or a blockage of some kind.

• **Diagonal** Dynamic angles and lines can express action, and could be uplifting, or illustrate a downward thrust. Perspective lines will draw the viewer into a focal area and create depth.

Top: **Estuary** (Carol Naylor, UK). Based on maps and aerial photography of the river Arun in West Sussex, UK, this stylized stitched textile has wonderful movement and use of colour. Centre and above: Photo of the Australian Centre for the Moving Image in Melbourne; linear tiles that are leaning forward.

When a symbol, line or shape is repeated several times in a composition, these dance across the surface. Pattern on the whole can be quite static but, when broken up into diagonal lines, these can jump across the surface. For instance, consider Bridget Riley's optical paintings. If you stand in front of one and look, after a while the lines begin to move. Op Art is full of optical illusions, with repeat circles or wavy lines creating a sense of movement. On a simpler level, movement can be suggested simply by placement – for example, a human form coming into or leaving a canvas will suggest movement.

UNITY

Making everything work together is the final – but not least – important aspect of a good design. Achieving this may seem like a tall order at the start, but as a stitched-textile artist, it is your main goal. The different elements – line, shape, space and tonal values – will all compete with one another for dominance, but until there is unity across the canvas, the piece is not finished. Making the final decision that the work is completed is also not easy, but the more we practise considering the elements and principles of design, the more we develop the ability to feel the work is right intuitively.

When planning a new design for a textile, I work through several compositions, usually as collage in paper, and view them on a design wall for a short time (taking too long to make a decision can be counterproductive). The one I usually choose is the first one I made. So I have learned that, even though several designs have been explored, and they all might work equally well, it is usually the first I make that will resonate with me. I often come back to the other designs and develop those as part of a series.

Above: The initial selection of papers used in this exercise.

You will need:

- A photograph of a favourite landscape with detail, or any image from your travels
- Reference material – colour photocopies, painted black-and-white photocopies, writings, and any painted, printed or dyed fabrics you would like to add
- A sheet of white A4 paper cut in two vertically to make a long, thin shape for the collage background, glue stick, ruler, craft knife, paper scissors
- Coloured pencils, chinagraph marker or oil pastels, and black felt pens for additional mark-making
- Camera, computer and colour inkjet printer
- One sheet of T-shirt transfer paper for white fabrics, baking parchment and iron, and a small amount of thin white cotton fabric for transferred images
- Sewing machine and threads, very thin wadding or sew-in soft interfacing, such as Vilene

Design Class 4
FOCUSING ON A LANDSCAPE

These long, thin, dramatic landscape collage compositions, created with painted papers and colour photocopies and based on your own personal theme, will give you more practice with finding focal points and centres of interest. Collages in paper can also be machine-stitched (with wadding and backing fabric added) or heat-transferred onto cloth.

Method

- Create a horizontal (or vertical) collage with between three and seven pieces of torn or cut paper arranged and glued onto one of your white paper backgrounds (see illustration below left). Crisp edges could suggest architecture, while torn, raw ones could express organic subjects. Once you have finished the first collage, make another.
- Trim a straight edge along the top of each collage, and piece them together so they become the full A4 page size again (illustration bottom left). Scan or photograph the result and download to your computer (illustration below right).
- Flip the on-screen image horizontally (once you transfer the image onto fabric, it will reverse back), especially if it includes writing or a recognizable place or person.

- Print out the flipped image in colour onto the T-shirt transfer paper with an inkjet printer (illustration below right). Cut the print in half and iron each half face down onto the cut pieces of cotton. Allow the required time for cooling (usually 20 seconds is enough, but read the manufacturer's instructions), then peel off the paper. The surface is usually very shiny, and this glossy finish can be removed by ironing a sheet of baking parchment over it several times until a matte surface is achieved.

- Layer the surface with thin wadding or interfacing and a backing fabric, and pin the sandwich ready for sewing. Stitch onto the surface, picking up information from the shapes and details in the collage image. You could also try stitching through the original paper collage, using interfacing and backing fabric.

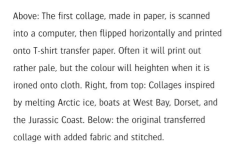

Above: The first collage, made in paper, is scanned into a computer, then flipped horizontally and printed onto T-shirt transfer paper. Often it will print out rather pale, but the colour will heighten when it is ironed onto cloth. Right, from top: Collages inspired by melting Arctic ice, boats at West Bay, Dorset, and the Jurassic Coast. Below: the original transferred collage with added fabric and stitched.

ABSTRACTION

Now you have a basic understanding of the elements and principles of design, it is time to go a step further and exaggerate the 'safe' compositions by playing with abstraction. With the use of collage, or sketches on a small scale (in your sketchbook), you can explore all the possibilities and learn how to leave your comfort zone and bend the rules in order to find your own personal style. Be expressive if you are making abstract art, and observe your personal reactions if you are the viewer. We will all respond differently to the same piece of work.

5

Left: **Shadows 2 (detail)** (Fenella Davies, UK). Subtle use of shape and colour with paint and textures is evident in this abstract art quilt. Right: Inspired by a painting by Frank Auerbach, this collage in painted papers has images of ancient textiles and a beach in new Zealand (Sandra Meech, UK).

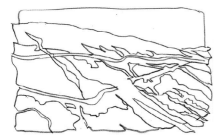

• **Make choices** You need to make early choices when creating abstract work. Will the piece incorporate figurative (realistic) elements, or be totally abstract (expressive or conceptual) in nature? What is the feeling that you want to engender?

• **Keep the information simple and dynamic** Many people do not realize that there is skill and effort behind the simple compositions of abstract art. It is all about selection – what is left in and what is eliminated. Just a suggestion of a shape, image or line can be enough for the piece to be interesting.

• **Make your expression dynamic** Using line, colour, value and shape – or a more subtle yet expressive composition may be the way forward.

• **Think laterally** Go back to the mind map (see page 15) in which you explored new directions within your subject. Any of these different aspects could inspire a new concept that could in turn influence an expressive or abstract approach.

(see page 15)

Hint

Sometimes, the theme that a textile artist has chosen might be difficult to understand at first. There might be a clue in the title or work in a series that the artist has made earlier. The artist statement will give a greater insight into inspiration, materials and techniques.

THE ABSTRACT COMPOSITION

An abstract composition can be approached from many directions. It might be inspired by realism, or by isolating a dynamic part of a reference image, or the approach might be instinctive, in which the artist explores texture, tone, line, shape and colour expressively.

Stylizing from a landscape

Try the following exercise to use realism as a jumping-off point for more abstract work.

Above: **Beach at West Bay** (Sandra Meech, UK). A simple collage with paper and images could easily become an appliqué stitched-textile piece.

Above: A landscape near Sedburgh, Cumbria, rendered as both simplified and stylized line drawings, and realistic and expressive colourways.

▶ *Begin with a favourite landscape photo for reference (a black-and-white copy will help to determine tones and contrasts). Draw or trace a simplified version in line, then another version with exaggerated features. A third sketch could take the abstraction further. Once you are happy with the drawing, photocopy it in black and white and explore different colourways – a realistic one and an expressive one. Perhaps flat areas could be collaged with painted papers. Consider how isolated areas from your design could become more stylized, while keeping the essence of the original. At this stage decide how it might be developed into a stitched piece – would appliqué or machine embroidery be appropriate?*

Isolation

Isolation or cropping of different areas from one source could be interesting, and different abstract areas from one source could be developed into a series. You have practised this technique with line and pattern in earlier exercises in this book, but the technique can be employed at any stage of development. Try this:

• Using a photograph of your choice – (the sample right is from hilltop houses in France), create a high-contrast black-and-white image on your computer to fill an A4 sheet of paper.
• Break the whole area into nine squares or rectangles. In the sample you can see how each section is different and has a graphic feel to it. When the shapes are simplified further, more abstract shapes appear.
• Use three or four of the images as a starting point for a series of textile pieces. In the case of the sample, these will be based on buildings.

Non-realistic expressive work

What might look like free expression, made with abandon, is usually carefully planned, with colour or shape picking up the flow of information across the surface and a well-established focal point that keeps the viewer's interest. Working in this way can open the door to finding your creative self. Emotional interpretations should always include some organisation to begin with but, with this framework in place, the artist can be spontaneous, intuitive and liberated. This way of working is in the realm of conceptual painting.

▶ *With acrylic, using a colour photograph to inspire you, paint brush 'marks' on cloth. Create surface texture with small bits of cut fabric bonded and stitched on top of your work. This could be an expressive way of using up leftover bits and pieces of fabric. Have some fun and don't worry about centres of interest – the colour will excite the viewer across the surface.*

Above: High-contrast black-and-white sections taken from a favourite photograph. One section was chosen for its interesting abstract shapes, and was then taken further in Photoshop. Below: **Embankment** (Sandra Meech, UK). London city lights inspired this abstract stitched collage.

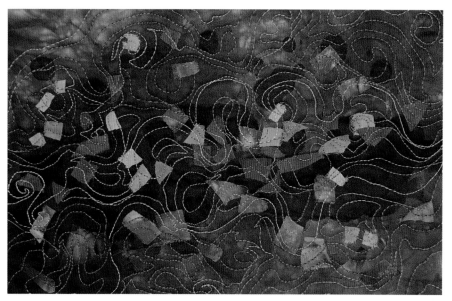

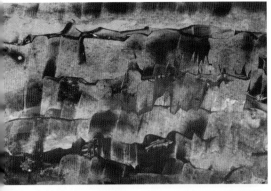

► *Make a palette-knife painting on canvas or thin card (see top left), creating quick explosions of colour and energy. This has to be done quickly to keep the colour pure and unmuddied. Use a photograph or any personal reference as a starting point for colour choices. Add acrylic paint to the left of the surface in daubs down the edge, then take a palette knife across from left to right. Jagged movements can create interest.*

► *Scan the whole painting or a section of it and make a jpeg file (or photograph your painting if you don't have a scanner.) Now print the image onto heat-transfer paper. Iron it face down onto your chosen cloth and use this as a fabric to be integrated into a larger textile work or developed as a stitched textile piece on its own (see photograph centre left).*

ABSTRACT ART INFLUENCES

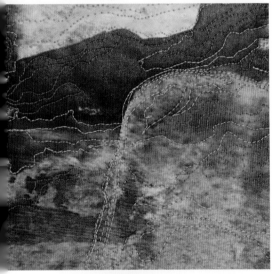

Visit contemporary art galleries to absorb as much as you can about abstract art. The more you look, the more you will become comfortable thinking in abstract terms when you see modern art. You will also become more confident about trying a new style for yourself. Take a notebook or sketchbook with you when you next visit a gallery, and sketch simple compositions that have been used. Don't worry – your work will not look derivative as you will be working in fabric and stitch.

Buy a book (or borrow one from the library) on any period of art from the Impressionists to present-day abstract or Expressionist painting to make a study of the work included. For the study of composition, look at the work of the Impressionists; for colour and movement, look at work by Van Gogh, Monet, Pissarro, Sisley and Cézanne; to study the use of shape and stylized form, look at the work of Picasso, Dali, Miró, Hundertwasser, Klimt, Lowry or Hockney. More Abstract Expressionists to study are Kandinsky, Pollock, de Kooning, Rothko and Richter. Also look at graphic-art styles – study the work of Warhol, Mondrian, Riley and Lichtenstein. To see more realistic abstract approaches, look at work by Georgia O'Keeffe, and Japanese art through the years. Select work you find particularly inspiring, and buy postcards to put up on your design wall for inspiration.

As you study the work of modern artists, you will find that you are always inexplicably drawn to a certain expressive style, and that you go back to that artist repeatedly.

Hint
Strong abstract shapes are always going to engage the viewer, especially in art quilting. Seen from a distance, they can be striking on a piece of work against a white wall (always imagine how your work will look in a gallery environment).

Above left: An isolated section from a quick palette-knife painting has been heat-transferred onto cloth and machine stitched to provide a small abstract stitched textile (Sandra Meech, UK). Left: A stitched textile collage inspired by an important contemporary British artist. Can you guess who it is? (Sandra Meech, UK).

Right: **St Paul's, Evening** (Sandra Meech, UK). A sunset impression of St. Paul's Cathedral, London was sketched onto poly-sateen fabric, coloured with transfer dyes, then machine stitched.

Design Class 5
ABSTRACT ART COMPOSITION

Exercise 1: Taking inspiration from art

For this exercise you will take inspiration from a small section of a piece of art, so that the pressure of creating your own design is removed. The process will set you free to have fun and not over-think the process, and the finished result will be a surprise. Artists such as Kandinsky, Picasso, Hundertwasser, Klimt and Miró could all work well as inspiration.

You will need

- A printout of a contemporary painting for exercise 1, and one of a still life for exercise 2
- L-shaped viewfinders
- White A4 plain paper and thin tracing paper
- Papers for collage
- Coloured pencils, thick felt-tip pens and oil pastels, glue stick, paper scissors, white chinagraph marker
- Craft knife, cutting board and metal ruler, pencils and eraser
- Medium interfacing (A4 size), backing fabric, pins
- Fabrics (dyed, stamped or commercial bali/batik-style cotton)
- Sewing machine and colourful machine threads

Method

- Isolate an interesting area on your chosen contemporary painting using the L-shaped viewfinders. Make your selection in a rectangular format, using the same proportions as the copy paper you are using as the background. Consider the centres of interest and how the information is placed so that the viewer's attention moves around the surface. Or consider an angled approach. Draw your cropped area onto the plain paper, enlarging it by eye to fill the page. This will act as a simple reference for adding collage to.
- Choose the collage papers that you think would work best and cut or tear sections, arranging them to follow the new design. Think about the background, too. Could one large printed page, perhaps with torn edges, pasted onto the plain paper, work? Your own colour and pattern choices may be very different from the original artist's work, which you are only using as a starting point. Glue sections onto the background, keeping it simple.
- Add detail with oil-pastel lines, black pen or a white chinagraph marker and, later, with machine stitch.

Below and right: a selection of collages inspired by the work of Frank Auerbach.

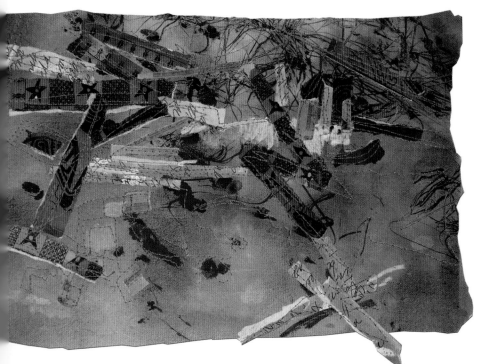

Exercise 2: Abstract flattened perspective

Techniques with flattened perspective have been used by artists and graphic designers for many years – look in house and garden magazines and you will, no doubt, find many examples. For this exercise, you will need to create a simple still-life arrangement using three to five items from around the house.

Method

- First, make a simple outline sketch of the still life. Consider light and shaded areas for tone (below left). Repeat the exercise, flattening areas and simplifying further. Try tracing the different elements of the still life and overlapping them (below, second left). These can be used in a quirky way. Flatten the table or background (below, third left) and play with the arrangement until you are satisfied. Perhaps you could try an example with the shapes floating randomly across the surface. Print black-and-white copies at different stages for reference, or add colour to them using colour pencils or a watercolour wash. The illustration below right was 'coloured in' using Photoshop for a deliberate flattened, graphic effect.

- A chosen design could be created in dyed, printed or stamped fabrics with either turned or raw-edge appliqué. A drawing of any decorative detail from the original could be added to the surface, which could inform stitch marks later.

Above: **Remembering Zoe** (Sandra Meech, UK), an image of favourite ceramic pieces.

Machine-stitching paper or transferred collages

Stitching through paper can be liberating – knowing that 'it's only paper' can allow you to stitch freely and expressively in the knowledge that no precious fabric is being wasted. Add a thin layer of wadding or a medium interfacing with a backing cloth and pin the layers together as a sandwich. Thread the machine as you would for fabric and set it for free-machine stitching using a darning foot. Don't think of the surface as paper, but enjoy creating interpretive stitch lines that extend beyond the information. A contrasting colour choice of thread can give extra impact. Work on an area no larger than A4 to allow for easy stitching.

Alternatively, the collage can be scanned as a jpeg file. Print this onto fabric using T-shirt transfer paper, then stitch expressively across the image, adding extra fabrics or wool, scrim, sheers or net embellishment. This could become a small prototype for a larger piece of work.

Above: a sketch based on the photograph, emphasizing its tonal aspects; with tracings overlaid for transparency; a line drawing with flattened perspective, which can be used as a master that could be then coloured with pencils or any other media; the final design has flat colour added in Photoshop. Right: **West Bay Shore** (Sandra Meech, UK). Paper or transferred fabric collages sometimes don't come to life until stitch is added.

COMPOSITION FOR STITCH

Composition is the orderly arrangement of all the elements in a piece of work, using the principles of design, to create a unified whole. This chapter is designed to help you review what you have learned so far and provide more suggestions about what makes a good composition. Recognizing these composition styles will be fundamental to evaluating and critiquing your own work (as well the work of others).

Left: **Spirit Eyes** (Sandra Meech, UK). A hand-stitched embroidery representing Inuit 'all-seeing' symbols, in a cruciform composition (see page 107). Right: **Meltdown 1** (Sandra Meech, UK). The first in this series based on the effects of global warming in the polar regions. The copper colour represents heat.

Above: The S-curve composition, seen in this photograph of Scottish shoreline and a painted photocopy of boats at West Bay, Dorset, with directional lines superimposed in white.

COMPOSITION STYLES

Shapes and their relationships to each other become the backbone of a surface composition in textiles – particularly in abstract designs. Thinking of the space we want to fill and the feeling we want to evoke are the first decisions in finding a strong composition.

Below is a list of composition suggestions. Many of these work for pictorial quilts, embroideries or collage compositions, while others will be more abstract in nature. Use this list as a resource when designing your compositions in stitched textiles, or to help you identify what other makers have done to achieve good compositions.

Sometimes, the elements of a composition – squares, circles, shapes or lines – will extend beyond the border or be very exaggerated or very subtle. This in itself can change the dynamic of a composition.

By now you will have accumulated many reference materials: colour copies, painted papers, magazine pages and dyed or painted fabrics for collage. Explore some of these composition styles for yourself using your reference material. Integrate any interesting compositions you produce into your bound sketchbook (see pages 28–29).

The 'S' curve

This is a classic compositional shape and can express great movement. It can be used on work that is horizontal or vertical in shape. The viewer is drawn from the base of the 'S' up to the edge and back again. The suggestion of the 'S' is made even if the curve goes off the edge. Curves of all kinds can create movement in a piece.

Above: **Black Water #3** (Judy Hooworth, Australia). A balanced composition incorporating movement through linear and curved shapes. Above right: 'X marks the spot' in this small textile piece. Right: Sketchbook pages explore curved shapes.

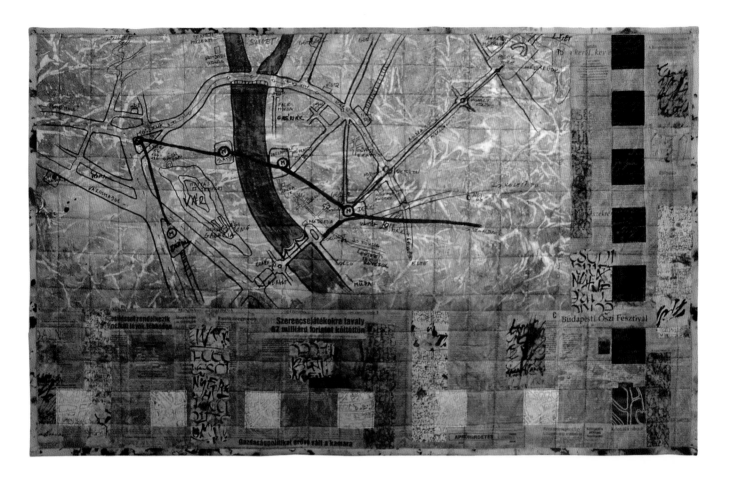

The cruciform format

Based on the rule of thirds (see page 35) when using horizontals and verticals, this is a classic composition style for both symmetrical and more abstract work. In the West, we read information from left to right, and real or suggested lines draw the viewer into the piece of work from the left straight to a focal point and beyond. There are two interesting cruciform (cross) compositions to consider. One has a central design with a high horizon line, while the other relies on placing a focal point at the intersection of one of the vertical and horizontal lines in the rule of thirds (see diagrams below left).

The 'L' shape

This compositional style is also classic. Originally deriving from the use of the cruciform shape and the rule of thirds, it can be exaggerated to be more dynamic, with an interesting area somewhere on one of the lines near the corner (see diagrams below).

Positioned at an angle, the 'L' becomes abstract. Use exaggerated 'L' shapes to hold the viewer's attention. Always make sure that diagonal lines are not positioned at the corner of your work, which will lead the eye out of the composition.

Top: **Subjective Mapping** (Eszter Bornemisza, Hungary) uses an L-shaped composition with a strong use of positive and negative shapes for added interest. Above: **By the Borderland VII** (Katriina Flensburg, Sweden) also uses an L-shaped format, with blocks and detail for interest. Left: diagrams of different composition styles, including curves, cruciform and L-shaped formats.

Top: **Algonquin Autumn** (Sandra Meech, UK). Strips of forest images move left to right across the surface. Above: Cape Cod beach at dusk, a high-horizon composition that shows details and textures on the shore. Right: Diagrams showing suggestions for different compositions: linear strips, high and low horizons, and combinations of block and linear shapes.

Horizontal and vertical lines

Employing horizontal and vertical lines and shapes is another classic composition style that is used in many art quilts and embroidered textiles (see page 60). High and low horizon (also related to the rule of thirds) creates a strong composition. All the parts of the design are unified as the colour or shape of the centre of interest leads the eye across the surface. This also applies to strips and stripes of varying widths across the surface, whether they are vertical or horizontal, but note that a strong horizontal line sometimes needs a vertical for contrast. A combination of lines and shapes can create a great number of exciting compositions that work in both realistic and abstract ways.

Diagonal shapes

Diagonal shapes can be dramatic and full of energy, as they accelerate movement across the surface. Care is needed in positioning them. Because they are powerful shapes, it is possible to shorten the ends or break the lines to slow the momentum. Horizontal and vertical lines or shapes crossing the diagonal composition will deflect some of its power.

▶ *Don't forget to try any of these composition examples in your sketchbook as small collages on a chosen theme, using your own reference material and colour choices.*

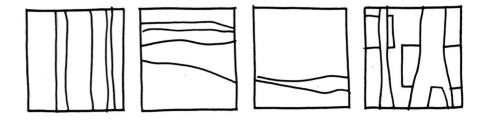

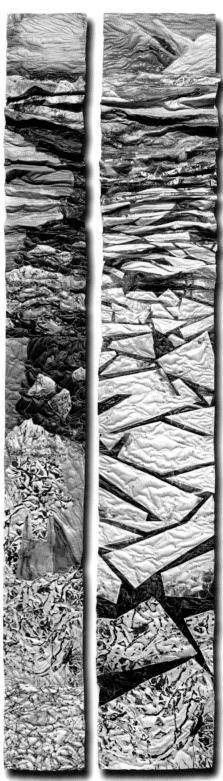

Above: **Ice Bay Morning** (Sandra Meech, UK). A painted line drawing was heat transferred in sections onto cotton, layered with Wireform and machine stitched for an 'off the wall' dimensional effect.

Above: **Floe Edge 1 and 2** (Sandra Meech, UK). Long, thin pieces stitched over Wireform.

   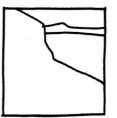 

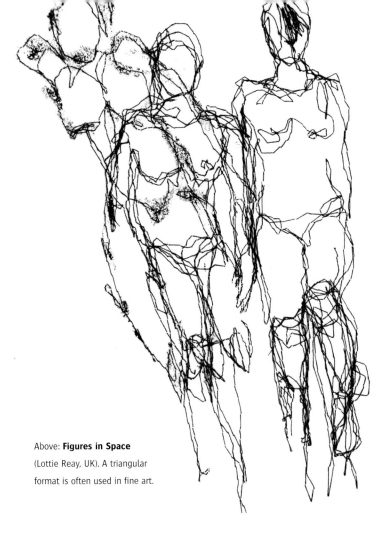

Above: **Figures in Space** (Lottie Reay, UK). A triangular format is often used in fine art.

Below left: The radiating shape of a loom at Farfield Mill, Cumbria, UK, and arches with vines create a central focus. Below: Still-life drawing (Sandra Meech, UK).

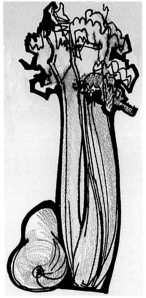

Triangular format

The centre of interest in the triangle is always at one of the angles. Used in still life, a triangular composition keeps the viewer's eye moving around the surface from one shape to another. Make sure one of the shapes used in the triangle is not too strong or close to the edge of the piece, so that the triangle is contained. The triangle can work well for an abstract still life with a grouping of three strong shapes, or compositions with flattened perspective.

Radiating shapes or lines

Radiating lines can create a strong composition – a principle that is evident in the New York Beauty quilt-design block. Radiating lines can be made with colour. The impression these lines make is so strong, in fact, that once the viewer has been directed to the centre, they lose interest. Varying the line widths or adding a weak line in a different direction can reduce the emphasis of the radiating lines. This composition can be effectively used in a landscape image – for example, as rows of crops where a high horizon line arrests the movement of the radiating lines.

Balanced shapes

This style of composition is like a see-saw balancing act of areas within the composition – large to small, light to dark, simple to detailed. Major masses in a composition can be balanced to create a dynamic design, but bear in mind that if the masses are too close in size, they can easily become boring and static.

▶ *Try creating several balanced compositions to see how far you can push the idea.*

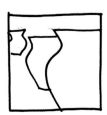

Above: Suggestions for triangular formats.

Above: Radiating shapes form dynamic compositions.

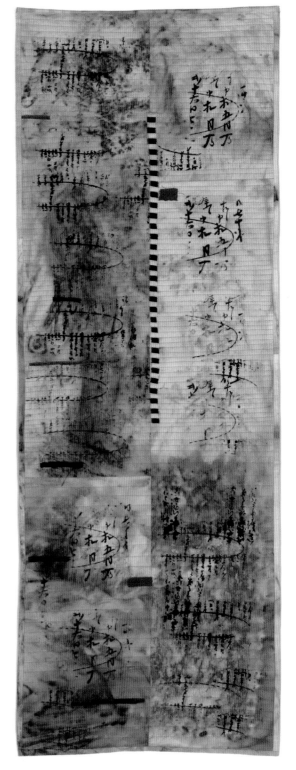

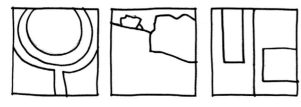

Above: Balanced shapes come in a variety of different forms.

Top left: **Oriental Pot 1 Blossom** (Hilary Beattie, UK). Above left: **Silent Woodlands** (Sandra Meech, UK). Above: **Ledger** (Jette Clover, Belgium) All three pieces, in their different ways, show a sense of balance with their placement of shapes and their use of colour.

Above: **Aphrodite** (Charlotte Yde, Denmark).
An intriguing use of the female figure.

Figure shapes

One strong, dynamic figure or shape can provide a wonderful focal point. A portrait or silhouette of a person can work when placed centrally or off to one side. Attention must be paid to the positive and negative shape that is created by the placement of the figure. Pictorial quilts are most dramatic when a single figure dominates. This compositional style can also be used for any object in a landscape – for instance, an image showing a single arched gateway can make a strong statement.

Circle shapes

The dynamic circle can bring interest to the surface of a textile work and, used as a central design feature, it can create an extremely strong composition – think of the Uncle Sam poster with the centralized finger pointing to the viewer. Used asymmetrically, in one of the four corners of the surface, a circle can add extra interest. Sometimes, the use of another focus of interest outside the circle can be appropriate.

Left: Circular and rectangular shapes contrast and yet balance each other (Sandra Meech, UK). Right: Two composition suggestions using circles.

Above: **Clear Waters** (Susan Strachan Johnson, Canada). This composition gives a feeling of movement.

Right: **Tourists** (Janet Cairney, UK). Strong figures create balance against the buildings.

Bending the rules

Once you have gained confidence in using different styles of composition, you can begin to extend or exaggerate many of the principles of design for dramatic effect. Visiting modern art galleries will provide you with opportunities to see real extremes in design. Always take a notebook with you and sketch some of these exaggerated compositions. Even if you don't immediately understand why they work, studying them over time might reveal how and why the artist has created a composition. With practice, you will be able to discern the rationale behind the simplest of paintings or pieces of textile art.

Left: Three figures together, as a group and with one isolated.

BORDER COMPOSITION

A border, or the lack of one, is an important factor in stitched textiles that can make or break the dynamics of the composition. Many quilters who have learned their skills through making bed quilts might continue using large borders in their contemporary quilts when they are not necessary. Borders can restrict a design, making a strong statement weak. On the other hand, some contemporary abstract pieces could benefit from an inferred border, just as a more figurative landscape in fabric could have more depth without one – think about how graphic some of the designs in African textiles are without any border treatment. It is always important to consider how you frame your composition from the start, not as an afterthought.

The symmetrical border

For quilters who started in textiles making traditional bed quilts, the border has a specific purpose – it allows for the main repeat of the 30cm (12in) blocks to remain on the top of the bed as the border drops to the side. In embroidery, a motif might have several borders or a repeated decorative detail on the edge of a tapestry, while a clothing garment can be finished with an edge.

It is often thought that by including a dominant border around a composition (or painting), the subject can be more clearly viewed – paintings in the world of art often had very large and ornate gilt frames. The block design on a bed quilt is also framed with a deep border that drapes down the sides of the bed.

Once a quilt comes off the bed and onto the wall, there is less of a need for this large, symmetrical frame. Often, the border on a contemporary textile can make what was potentially a dynamic arrangement boring and mediocre. If borders are to be used in quilting or textiles then yes, they can provide a frame for focus, but they need to be integral to the overall composition. A symmetrical border can be made more interesting with the use of broken colour, diagonal lines or shapes that relate to the design within the border.

The asymmetrical border

Using an asymmetrical border can create very interesting results, and contemporary quilters often use this more abstract method to give a different focus to the whole piece.

Opposite: **The Quarryman's Quilt** (Clyde Oliver, UK) explores a symmetrical border treatment with an unconventional material – slate.

Top: **Back Street in Florence** (Susan Strachan Johnson, Canada). The graffiti panel is central to the bordered detail in the rest of this stitched textile. Above: Silk Road 2 (Dwayne Wanner, Canada). The smaller blocks provide a frame for the larger, more central one, with the addition of lively, colourful, directional lines that create movement.

Left: **Running in the Tate** (Johnnene Maddison, Canada). The focus is highlighted with an implied border that is full of activity and detail.
Below: **Shoreline** (Susan Strachan Johnson, Canada). No border is necessary in this painted stitched textile series that shows colours, textures and reflections by the lake.

Shape elements in the border

Simply put, employing shapes that have extended into the border from the main body of the work is an excellent way of inviting viewers into the composition. They will enter the piece from the left or any other strong leading point, and the shapes within the frame could also form a directional line to reinforce this guide.

See the design class about abstract borders on pages 118–120 for more ideas.

The implied border

Perhaps only a suggestion of a frame is all that is necessary to make a stitched-textile piece work. This can be as subtle as you want, and can be done with colour, tones and values, piecing, painting or stitching. You can add an asymmetrical border and cut into it with an overlapping part of the centre. This way, the focus area expands into the muted border.

Mounting a group of small textile works on a large format will imply a border to them all – the eye will read the background as a border (see the quilt on page 115). This can be effective when working in a series. Sometimes, the shapes of the pieces do not need to be all the same.

No border

This is probably the preferred art-quilt treatment. When textile art is competing with fine-art painting and mixed media for exhibition space, creating the most dynamic composition from a fine art point of view is a big consideration. Without a border treatment, the viewer is invited into the surface without obstacle.

Above: **Broken** (Amarjeet Nandhra, UK). No border is needed in this strong, dynamic piece, with the focus being drawn to the line in gold. Left: **Black Water #4** (Judy Hooworth, Australia) No borders are necessary in this dynamic series of evocative work that explores the movement of water.

Above: The original reference photograph
for this exercise.

You will need
- White copy paper, glue stick, scissors,
  ruler
- A fine-nibbed permanent pen and
  coloured pencils
- Reference material: a selection of colour
  and black-and-white photocopies on a
  personal theme, painted papers and
  magazine pages, and a reference image

EXPLORING BORDER DESIGN

Borders can help to frame our stitched textiles, whether they take the form of quilts,
embroidered pieces or mixed-media pieces. Sometimes, work is framed in such a subtle
way that the conventional border is hardly evident at all.

Exercise 1: Borders from a reference source
This method provides a very quick way of producing a contemporary composition from a
real-life subject. Although symmetrical in nature, the borders on the finished compositions
are contemporary in feeling. In this exercise you will isolate sections of an image or collage
and abstract them to form the basis of a final stitched textile work. It is best to work with a
photographic reference to begin with.

Method
- Make 4 copies of your photographic reference.
- Select a 7.5cm (3in) square-shaped detail, and a 2.5cm × 10cm (1in × 4in) rectangular-
  shaped detail from the image. Cut 1 square and 4 identical rectangles. Note the detail at
  one end of the rectangle.
- Position the square on a piece of copy paper with the first rectangle placed on top, as
  shown below. Find the second rectangle, rotate it as shown below, and place it on the
  right-hand side. Continue with the final two rectangles, rotating them in the same
  direction, and glue the square and rectangles in place.

Looking at the samples for this exercise, you can see that the essence of the original image
is evident, but the finished piece has a contemporary feel. Two samples can be seen below
right – both were photocopied and coloured with pencil for different effects. A further
isolated section (perhaps long and thin, as shown), could inspire a more abstract piece.

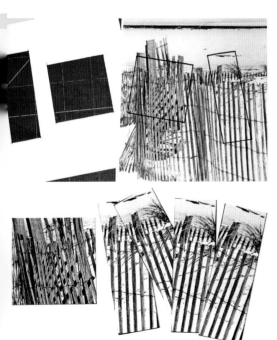

Above: Cut one square and four identical rectangles
for this exercise.

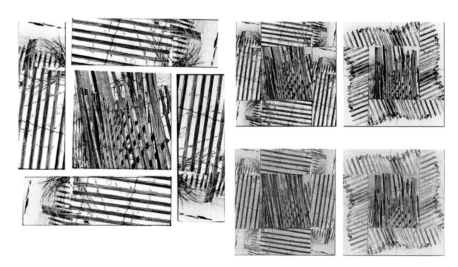

Above: Use the square for the centre and the
rectangles for the border.

Exercise 2: Framing an area of interest

Method

For this exercise you will work in paper, but all samples could become a basic design for a fabric composition.

You will need a 7.5cm (3in) square of detail from a colour photocopy image on a theme, or from a magazine reference. Find 10cm (4in) and 13cm (5in) square pieces of painted paper to complement the first square. Some pattern or texture might be interesting, but keep it relatively plain (see the example right).

- Arrange these squares in a) a symmetrical way, b) with the central focus in one corner, c) with the middle square set at an angle, and d) with a more abstract arrangement.
- Create more variations. Photograph or scan each sample for future reference. The symmetrical examples will be pleasing, but boring; the diagonal square will be more interesting, and the off-centre designs more dynamic and abstract. Perhaps one of these designs could be taken further in fabric and stitch on a small scale. It's worth also thinking about using L-shaped viewfinders to isolate a more abstract section of one of the compositions.

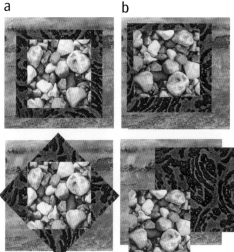

a   b

c   d

Exercise 3: Rotating borders

This is one of my favourite border exercises. The source of inspiration is a colour photocopy, and choosing the best image is important – make sure there is contrast of shape or colour in the image.

Method

- Photocopy your chosen image in colour. Find a 13cm (5in) square area and, using the template suggestion below, draw successive borders 2.5cm (1in) wide around a central 5cm (2in) square. When your image is cut out, begin with the inner border and rotate it once to the right around the central square.
- Rotate the next border twice to the right, then the next 3 times, and finally the outside border once to the right. The new design will have balance and will be symmetrical in nature, but with a contemporary twist. In the last version, the outside border remains in the same orientation at it was originally. This way the viewer sees a recognizable reference in the centre and the outside as the attention moves in and out. Consider how you could do this in fabric appliqué.

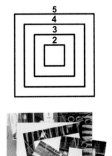

Exercise 4: Using transparency as a border

This exercise could be done using a simple collage based on images and painted paper on a personal theme.

Method

• Once you have created a simple collage, find a square or rectangular area that will become the main focus in the composition. Now cut the selected area out of thin tracing paper and lay it onto the surface to create the effect. The whole surface area can now be cropped to make the piece appear like an art quilt. Now try cutting out a different area from tracing paper to give a new composition. If you wish you can scan your image into a computer and darken the background using Photoshop to leave the focal area brighter. Perhaps this could give you ideas for using sheer fabrics to diffuse detail and lighten or darken the background.

Exercise 5: Fine-line border fun

This last exercise could be the one border treatment that will take your work further – borders, whether seen or implied, play an important role in contemporary stitched textiles.

Method

• Keeping to a simple approach on your personal theme, create two or three small collages.
• With thin strips of paper in a contrasting colour, glue a border in place. Remember these 'framing' lines do not have to be parallel to the edges and can be set at an angle.
• Scan one of the collages and consider how it might be cropped further to create different shapes, or set at an angle. Many of your experiments could suggest ideas for an art quilt.

Top: Experiments using transparency. Above: Using thin strips of paper to create borders.

TAKING THE NEXT STEP INTO STITCH

One of the most important steps for a textile artist is from the small-scale collage that evokes everything you want in a composition – strength of focus, dynamic movement, colour contrasts – to a larger-scale textile piece. When it comes to determining how to make it larger, there is no easy and direct answer, because everyone comes to this stage with a different set of stitching and piecing skills, perhaps from different fabric and cloth disciplines. Everyone has different levels of experience or preferred working methods. When students ask me how they can start to make large-scale textile work from a small collage, I tell them they have to ask themselves about their own particular project and stitch experience, and address the following issues.

Size and scale

What size do you want the piece to be? Will it work if enlarged from a 20 × 25cm (8 × 10in) collage to a large art quilt? It might be a good idea to find out if your composition works as a middle-sized piece first. The feeling or essence of the collage will be changed when re-created with fabric, and on a larger scale. Photograph a composition at the collage stage and, on the computer, place it on a white background. Now position a person nearby for scale purposes – you will get a sense of how it would enlarge in a gallery environment, and you'll also get an idea of how well the composition works on that scale.

Materials and fabrics

The detail on the surface of a small-scale collage will change when it is taken larger. Consider how you would get a similar effect to the surface detail on a larger scale, perhaps by painting or stamping cloth, or screen-printing it. Perhaps the effect of the surface detail you are trying to re-create on a large scale could be achieved with raw-edge appliqué? Projecting an enlarged image on a wall using a digital projector could also help you identify which methods you need to use in order to create the surface pattern you are after.

Stitch as line

You need to establish how to use stitch on a large scale in order to achieve the types of lines you want in your composition. If any interpretive 'marks' are very large (they might be made with pieces of rolled or bonded fabric, textured wool or any other heavier materials), they will need to be stitched or applied separately.

Right: **Arctic Memories 1 and 2** (Sandra Meech, UK). These small pieces work well as stitched-textile pieces, but different materials and techniques would need to be employed if the same compositions were to be enlarged to become large-scale art quilts.

Exhibiting potential

Your choice of materials should be appropriate for shipping and hanging so you have every opportunity to exhibit your work. It is important to consider any problems first before embarking on some styles of dimensional work. If your work must be posted, it will be easier to do so if it is rolled rather than mounted on a frame. Also consider the following:

- **Concept and theme** Are there any unfamiliar techniques that might be worth investigating before you start to create a larger piece? For example, a piece about memory loss could include working with faded images that have been screen-printed or transfer-dyed onto sheer fabrics. On the same theme, machine stitching through soluble materials can be used to create an irregular lace effect to express the idea of nerve endings that don't quite meet. The contrast from full images from life to faded, almost nonexistent distressed marks could also express this theme. On any theme, there might be new skills to be explored or familiar techniques to be reviewed.

- **Developing a series** You should be able to scale and enlarge most of your sample collages quite easily. This could result in several middle-sized textile pieces that could be developed into a series.

Left: **Bulles-bleues, Bulles-roses** (Anne Worringer, France). Working in a specific series or style, as seen here, will make work more recognizable. Below: **Meltdown 1, 2, 3** (Sandra Meech, UK).

STITCH EFFECTS FOR COMPOSITION

Often, a stitched-textile piece will be designed and stitched, but lacks something to keep the viewer's eye flowing across the piece. Apart from colour choices that can link two sections of a piece to allow the eye to move across the surface, there are shapes that can become part of the pattern that encourage one area to be linked to another.

The darning stitch
This simple stitch mark can be done by hand in a gentle curve that makes its way through the entire piece and will subconsciously take the viewer's eye across the surface. It could be in a strong colour, or in a subtle one, so that it is not instantly seen, but picked up randomly or subliminally.

Bullets
Stitched bullets can help to take one's eye across the piece. Bullets can be created with a stationary satin stitch. Group the bullets randomly, with a concentration of them in a focal area, or spread them rhythmically across the surface.

Linking lines and shapes
When the division between two areas in a composition is too strong, small linking stitch lines or thin rectangular shapes (sometimes in a strong colour) can moderate the division between them. Because they can be vertical or horizontal, and at right angles to the join, they will blend into the design, but suggest a link between areas. Lines or shapes are often made in odd-number groupings.

'X' marks the spot
These are excellent mini focal points when a piece clearly needs more emphasis in certain areas. These, like the strong cruciform shape (see page 107), will automatically bring the viewer's eye into the work and have it rest in an important area. A small series of 'x's can also be used to join two separate areas, linking them together for unity.

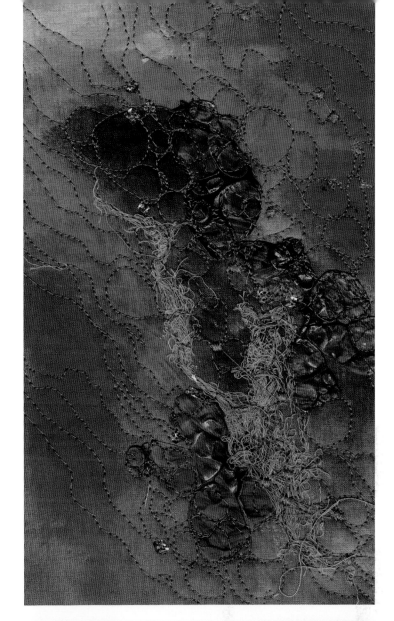

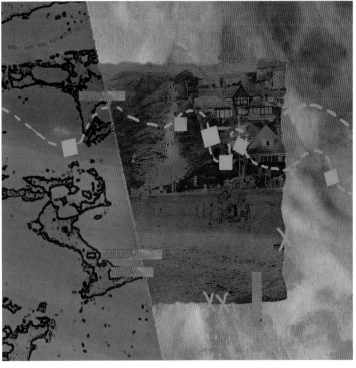

Top right: **Red with Blue Bullets** (Sandra Meech, UK). Could blue satin-stitch 'marks' create additional movement across the surface?
Right: A stitch sample showing linking and joining effects, including a simple darning stitch across the surface, bars placed to join sections together, 'bullets' in squares of fabric or satin stitch as points of focus; and crosses in stitch. Only one or two of these effects should be used in a finished textile piece, to prevent your work looking cluttered.

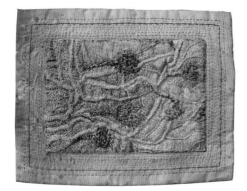

STITCH BY DESIGN

Everyone will be making their own unique textile piece, developed from a personal subject, inspired by different colours, materials, surface-design techniques and composition styles. The design that stitch will take should also be a consideration from the start. Below are some suggestions for how to begin.

- Stitching directly into paper collage is a good way in which to experiment with free-motion embroidery and interpretive machine stitch. Knowing that it is only paper you are working on – and not an expensive or precious piece of fabric – can be a freeing experience that allows you to just 'go for it'.

- Consider planning a completely different design for the stitching line than that suggested by the fabric surface detail. For example, the surface might be made up of straight, bold, architectural lines that are angled, sharp and vertical. The stitching lines, whether made by hand or machine, could be just the opposite, to reflect the curves of glass reflections that are wavy and organic, or the diagonal lines that flow across the surface. The contrast may not be evident from a distance but once the viewer looks more closely, the stitch will become an integral part of the whole piece.

- With any contemporary patterned commercial fabrics – Bali- and batik-style materials or handmade stamped or painted surfaces – you can be very expressive with your stitch marks. Use the design, pattern or shapes in the fabric as inspiration for stitch, and continue with the design in stitch beyond the fabric edge.

- If using imagery, consider extending the detail of the photo or shape beyond the fabric edge. This will also link shapes on the surface together.

Above: **Sea World** (Sybil Rampen, Canada) (detail shown below). Lines of movement are obvious in this piece, but on closer inspection the stitch marks show greater energy in the negative areas. It is easy to imagine the wind blowing seeds everywhere.

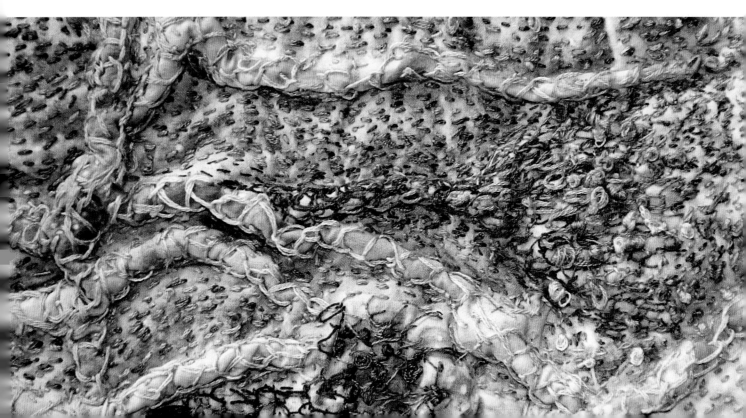

Above: **Posterwall from the Tate, London**
(Sandra Meech, UK) A glimpse of the Thames
through hoardings and posters on walls in
Southwark, London.

CONCLUSION

When we first see an art quilt or stitched-textile piece, we notice the 'wow factor' – the
immediate feeling that is conveyed. Turning the corner in a gallery or at a large exhibition
and experiencing that slight intake of breath when I see a stunning piece of work is a
wonderful sensation. We can soon establish whether the work is realistic, abstract,
expressive, or decorative but, beyond that, we want it to be balanced and yet exciting,
with a challenging use of colour or an expressive use of shape. Will the composition
evoke emotions? Will the arrangement be active – energetic and dynamic, with evidence
of movement – or will it be peaceful and passive? A well constructed composition can't
have all of those things at once, but understanding what makes a good design – the basic
elements and principles of design – will help us identify a successful result.

In all textile-art disciplines there is a need for composition or structure. How the
painter explores contrast, form or line on the surface of a painting is no different to how
a contemporary textile artist arranges areas of fabric, texture and stitch. Did the early
painters have a formula for good composition? Not at first, but, over time, the study of
design and composition has brought together several 'rules' that we can practise and utilize.
Sometimes, these rules are stretched and unrecognizable in the finished piece, yet the
composition still works well. We can strive to find a sense of harmony in our own work,
but we still need to challenge ourselves and go beyond our normal boundaries
sometimes – consider how Salvador Dali pushed balance and design to the limits with his
work.

A good composition has to engage viewers at a distance before they come closer and see
the fine use of stitch, the textures or fabric choices. If attention has not been given to the
good use of colour, shape and form to begin with, viewers will not come closer for that
second look.

Coming from an art and graphic design background has been a great help in my own
stitched textiles, but I know that design does not come naturally and easily to most of us.
It is my hope that, by working with this book, you will find new confidence in your own
personal journey in textile design and composition.

125

DESIGN GLOSSARY

Abstract Based on colour and form rather than realistic depiction.

Acrylic paint A quick-drying, permanent, colourfast paint which can be used on fabric for stitch. Watered-down acrylic paint on cotton is effective when used with Bondaweb to create interesting effects.

Brusho and Koh-i-noor Bright water-based dyes, used for painting paper. Koh-i-noor comes in a palette of 12 colours that is perfect for travelling. Wax resist and bleach work well with these dyes. Procion dyes, though more often used on fabric, will give a similar effect on paper.

Canvas A heavy cotton fabric which supports acrylic or oil paint. The term can also refer to the whole surface of a piece of art.

Collage An artistic composition of materials and objects that have been pasted onto a surface, often with unifying colour and line. In fine art, collage was popularized by Picasso and Braque.

Composition The arrangement and combination of different elements in a piece of art. Composition is important for enabling the viewer to engage with the work.

Contemporary Of the present time. Textile work that is being done with the latest methods and techniques could be considered contemporary, and today's styles vary enormously, from realist to expressive.

Cubism The art style developed by painters such as Picasso and Braque, which breaks down natural forms into geometric shapes.

Design 1. To make drawings, sketches and plans; 2. To plan the form or structure of an object; 3. To organise the formal elements in a work of art to form a composition.

Digital camera A camera that produces digital images that can be stored and displayed on a computer or printed onto paper or fabric.

Dyes Popular types of dye include Procion for natural fabrics or paper, and disperse dyes, transfer dyes and other heat-set dyes for manmade fabrics such as polyesters.

Elements of design The 'design tools' used to make a good composition – line, shape, space, value, colour, texture and pattern.

Expressionism An art movement, dating from the early 20th century, in which realism was replaced by an emotional connection to the subject. Paintings were abstract, with subjects and colours distorted.

Fibonacci sequence. This sequence of numbers, in which each number in the sequence is the sum of the previous two (i.e., $0+1=1$, $1+1=2$, $2+1=3$, $3+2=5$, $5+3=8$, $8+5=13$, $13+8=21$ and so on) occurs in nature – in the veins of a leaf, the spiral in a conch shell or the arrangement of sunflower seeds in the centre of a flower.

Figurative Art that illustrates a realistic subject (despite the name, subject matter does not have to include the human form).

Foreshortening The optical illusion of a sense of distance as the size of the subject (on a two-dimensional plane) is made smaller.

Golden mean or **golden section** A ratio of 8:13, which gives a pleasing sense of proportion and balance when used in art and architecture.

Graphic design The practice of combining text and images to communicate an effective message, as seen in magazines, brochures, books, billboards, posters and website design.

Health and safety Safety is an important consideration with many materials used in this book. Dye powders, including Procion, disperse, transfer and Brusho (paper) dyes can be airborne when mixed, so a mask is essential. Fumes from heat-transfer methods can also be harmful. Always work in a well-ventilated space.

Horizon line The imaginary line at eye level when viewing a landscape, where the vanishing point or points are located. In perspective, the horizon line should not be confused with the line where the land and sky meet, which could be higher or lower than eye level.

Impressionism A style of painting, developed in France in the late 19th century, that used broken colour to give an atmospheric, visual impression of the subject. In Impressionism, light and the spectrum of bright colour is depicted in short brushstrokes that appear broken and incoherent when viewed closely, but when seen from a distance recombine in the viewer's eye. This is known as an 'optical mixture'.

Interfacing A non-woven fabric, used mainly in the clothing or garment industry, can be used in textile art as a thin wadding or backing layer for the application of mixed materials including paper, plastics and fabric. Very stiff interfacings, such as pelmet Vilene, give a firm backing to wall-hung pieces, boxes or book covers.

L-shaped viewfinders These are useful for isolating a chosen area in an image and pulling it out as an abstract.

Mindmap A diagram to represent words, ideas and observations arranged around a central word that represents a theme.

Mixed media The use of a mix of two or more types of media, for example watercolour, gouache and acrylic paint with paper, metals, plastics, fabric and stitch.

Morris, William A British textile designer, artist and writer, associated with the Pre-Raphaelite and Arts and Crafts movements of the 19th century.

Negative space The space around an object, rather than the shape itself.

Perspective The way of representing a subject to give the impression of depth on a flat surface. In linear perspective, receding parallel lines seem to converge at a point on the horizon.

Photographic transfer methods There is a variety of methods for transferring photographs onto fabrics, including an acrylic medium called Picture This, a liquid called Bubble Jet Set that saturates cotton to enable it to be used in an inkjet printer, and heat-transfer methods using T-shirt papers. There is plenty of information in books and on the Internet for these techniques.

Photoshop Elements Affordable photo-editing software, which offers digital effects. Picasa or Photoscape are available free on the Internet and are also worth a look.

Realism An artistic style that takes inspiration from everyday life. A combination of some real detail with abstract backgrounds can be effective in contemporary stitched textiles.

Rule of thirds The system of dividing a plane into thirds to create a centre of interest and harmonious effect over the surface.

Screenprinting A technique in which fabric or paper is printed through a mesh screen.

Tone/value The lightness or darkness of any areas of the subject, regardless of colour. In colour terms, 'tone' can be used when examining hues that are naturally lighter than others, e.g. yellow compared with purple.

Typography The art of typeface design and the way it is laid out on a page for visual effect. Letters on their own can be beautiful symbols, and the use of words in textile art is a valuable way to engage the viewer.

Wireform A thin wire mesh that can be used as a fourth layer in a quilt, enabling it to be manipulated for dimension. However, thin mesh can dull sewing-machine needles quickly.

BIBLIOGRAPHY

Books on design

Aimone, Steven. *Design! A Lively Guide to Design Basics for Artists & Craftspeople.* Lark Books, 2004

Albert, Greg. *The Simple Secret to Better Painting.* North Light Books, 2003

Atkinson, Jennifer, Holly Harrison and Paula Grasdal. *Collage Sourcebook: Exploring the Art and Techniques of Collage.* Apple Press, 2004

Bothwell, Dorr and Marlys Mayfield. *Notan: The Dark-Light Principle of Design.* Dover Publications, 1991

Brommer, Gerald. *Collage Techniques: A Guide for Artists and Illustrators.* Watson-Guptill, 1994

Faimon, Peg and John Weigand. *The Nature of Design: How the Principles of Design Shape Our World.* How Design Books, 2004

Genders, Carolyn. *Sources of Inspiration.* A & C Black, 2008

Jerstorp, Karin and Eva Kohlmark. *The Textile Design Book.* Lark Books and A & C Black, 1988

La Plantz, Shereen. *Cover to Cover: Creative Techniques for Making Beautiful Books, Journals and Albums.* Lark Books, 1998

Laury, Jean Ray. *Imagery on Fabric: A Complete Surface Design Handbook.* C & T Publishing, 1997

Oei, Loan and Cecile de Kegel. *The Elements of Design: Rediscovering Colours, Textures, Forms and Shapes.* Thames & Hudson, 2002

Patterson, Neil. *Design and Composition Secrets of Professional Artists.* International Artists Publishing, 2001

Peterson, Bryan. *Learning to See Creatively: Design, Color and Composition in Photography.* Amphoto Books, 2003

Pipes, Alan. *Foundations of Art and Design.* Laurence King Publishing, 2003

Samara, Timothy. *Design Elements: A Graphic Style Manual.* Rockport Publishers, 2007

Other books I would recommend

Ash, Bethan. *Instinctive Quilt Art: Using Improvisational Techniques to Create Vibrant Art Quilts.* Batsford, 2011

Greenlees, Kay. *Creating Sketchbooks for Embroiderers and Textile Artists.* Batsford, 2005

Holmes, Cas. *The Found Object in Textile Art.* Batsford, 2010

Johnson, Ann. *The Quilter's Book of Design.* The Quilt Digest Press, 1997

Kinard, Lyric. *Art + Quilt: Design Principles and Creativity Exercises.* Interweave Press, 2009

Meech, Sandra. *Contemporary Quilts: Design, Surface and Stitch.* Batsford, 2003

Meech, Sandra. *Creative Quilts: Inspiration, Texture and Stitch.* Batsford, 2006

Meech, Sandra. *Connecting Art to Stitch.* Batsford, 2009

Morioka, Adams and Terry Stone. *Color Design Workbook.* Rockport Publishers, 2008

Schwarz-Smith, Lura and Kirby C. Smith. *Secrets of Digital Quilting.* C & T Publishing, 2010

Twinn, Janet. *Colour in Art Quilts.* Batsford, 2011

Wolfrom, Joen. *Adventures in Design.* C & T Publishing, 2011

Zeibarth, Charlotte. *Artistic Photo Quilts.* C & T Publishing, 2009

SUPPLIERS

UK

Seawhite of Brighton
Tel: 01403 711633
www.seawhite.co.uk

Art Van Go
Tel: 01438 814946
www.artvango.co.uk

Rainbow Silks
Tel: 01494 862929
www.rainbowsilks.co.uk

Colourcraft UK
Tel: 0114 242 1431
www.colourcraftltd.com

Freudenberg Nonwovens
Tel: 01422 327 900
www.nonwovens-group.com

Whaleys (Bradford) Ltd
Tel: 01274 576718
www.whaleys-bradford.ltd.uk

Photo Paper Direct
Tel: 0208 440 6115
www.photopaperdirect.com

USA

Dick Blick Art Materials
Tel: 1-800-723-2787
www.dickblick.com

Dharma Trading Company
Tel: 1-800-542-5227
www.dharmatrading.com

Pro Chemical & Dye, Inc
Tel: 1-800-228-9393
www.prochemical.com

Printonit
Tel: 1-701-663-4155
www.printonit.com

Canada

G & S Dyes and Accessories Ltd
Tel: 1-800-596-0550
www.gsdye.com

Groups

Quilt Art
www.quiltart.eu

Studio 21 Textile Artists
www.studio21textileart.co.uk

Connections Fibre Artists
www.connectionsfibreartists.com

The Quilters' Guild of the British Isles
www.quiltersguild.org.uk

Embroiderers' Guild UK
www.embroiderersguild.com

Sandra Meech
www.sandrameech.com
www.sandrameech-art.blogspot.com

INDEX

Award-winning quilt artist **Sandra Meech** is an international teacher and
lecturer who works with quilting, embroidery and textile groups in the UK
and abroad. Originally from Canada, she has a background in graphic design
and art, and is renowned for her themes inspired by the Arctic landscape and
the Inuit, the effects of global warming on woodlands and forests, and
buildings and urban living. She is a member of Quilt Art, an international
group of contemporary quilt artists, and exhibits widely in the UK, Europe
and North America, where many of her quilts are in private collections.
She is the author of *Contemporary Quilts: Design, Surface and Stitch*,
Creative Quilts: Inspiration, Texture and Stitch, and *Connecting Art to Stitch*,
also published by Batsford. To find out more about the author, go to
www.sandrameech.com.

Also available from Batsford:

Connecting Art to Stitch
Sandra Meech
9781906388102

Creative Quilts: Inspiration, Texture and Stitch
Sandra Meech
9780713490060

Colour in Art Quilts
Janet Twinn
9781849940009

To receive regular email updates on forthcoming Anova titles, email
update@anovabooks.com with your area of interest in the subject field.

Visit www.anovabooks.com for a full list of our available titles.